I0450604

Five Times: The Best Was Last

Five Times: The Best Was Last

Kaysee Smalley

Writers Club Press
San Jose New York Lincoln Shanghai

Five Times: The Best Was Last

All Rights Reserved © 2001 by Kaysee Smalley

No part of this book may be reproduced or transmitted in any form or by any means, graphic, electronic, or mechanical, including photocopying, recording, taping, or by any information storage retrieval system, without the permission in writing from the publisher.

Writers Club Press
an imprint of iUniverse.com, Inc.

For information address:
iUniverse.com, Inc.
5220 S 16th, Ste. 200
Lincoln, NE 68512
www.iuniverse.com

ISBN: 0-595-17493-0

Printed in the United States of America

Dedicated to my dear husband
For the rest of our life,
From your devoted wife
Kaysee Smalley

ACKNOWLEDGMENTS

I would like to thank my Mom. Ardella Boyer for the love she gave me. Thanks to my husband for the time, space, confidence and the love to write this book; my biggest motivator and supporter are my husbands, Eric. To my Dad, Lugene Reed for the love he showed me before his' death. At the top of my list, are my children, Dermaine Mitchell, Sherry Conrad and Shirley J. Mitchell, who I will miss.

INTRODUCTION

All my life, all I ever wanted is to be love. My Mother divided her love by ten. She gave birth to nine girls: Sara, Carolyn, Barb, Linda, Jade, Cindy, Brenda, Rachel and of course, me (Ellen). She bore only one son: Alton, we called him Al. Mom did not ever have all of her children together at one time. This was due to the age gaps and with her being married several times. By her first husband, Mr. Coleman the first child, Sara was born. Mr. Coleman was much older than Mom was. Mr. Coleman being in the military, he transferred often to different city causing them to be apart often. During one of Mr. Coleman's tours, he met a woman and eventually moves in with her. While Mr. Coleman was writing to Mom and his sister, the letters are place in the wrong envelopes by mistake, which is how Mom found out about his living arrangements with the other woman. She divorced him soon afterwards. When Sara had turned ten years of age, she went to live with her Father. By then, Mom had remarried. She had become Mrs. August Jenkins. Within three years, she bore three daughters with Mr. Jenkins: Carolyn, Barb, and Linda. He to, was in the military and met someone else while separated from Mom during his tour. Mom was pregnant with Linda, the youngest.

Once Mom had approached him about the other woman, he became abusive physical and mentally toward Mom. After Mom gave birth to her baby and is well enough to travel she will take her three daughters to Texas. Mom lived with her sister long enough to save enough money to get her own apartment.

Two years passed before Mom met Mr. Larry Rich, her third husband. Together they have two children, a son, Alton Larry Rich and a daughter, Ellen May Rich. Mom and Dad were together for four years when Dad began to get restless. Dad, before committing adultery, got out of the marriage. He did not want to hurt Mom, by cheating while still with her. She was very bitter with Dad for many years. They did eventually become friends.

Mom met Mr. Middleton, the boxer, and two years after her divorce from Dad. They were in the third year of their marriage when Mom bore two daughters with Mr. Middleton: Jade the oldest and Cindy. While she was in her seventh month of pregnancy, Mr. Middleton quit his job. He got really upset when Mom asked him why. He used his skills as a boxer, punching her in the stomach. She pressed charges against him and filed for a divorce. Due to the seriousness of the attack the divorce got dissolved quickly. She delivered Cindy soon after the attack without complications. At the age of six years old, I promised Mr. Middleton that I would kill him when I got older. Even though I was only six years old, I could not have been any more serious.

A month later, I asked to go live with my Dad. Mom agreed to let me go stay with my Dad but I will stay most weekends with her. I remained with my Dad until I reached the age of twelve years old. Dad thought that would be the appropriate age, saying she will be able to tell me the things all young girls that age should know.

Carolyn and Barb have gone to Chicago, all ready to live with their Father and finish their last year of High School. Mom only has Linda, Al, Jade, Cindy and myself at home now. Linda would be leaving next summer to join Barb and Carolyn in Chicago.

The summer is here; Linda is preparing to leave for Chicago. Mom has met Mr. James Bower. They have been dating for six months. He is always at our house when he got off work. Mom would not allow him to stay over night. Instead, she would go to his house for the weekend, taking the youngest children with her. Al and I would stay home. I did not like Mr. James much but I tolerated him because he is good to Mom. She deserved this much: after all she has been through.

I'm now eight years' old. Mom is still dating Mr. James. She is also expecting a new baby any day now. Everyone's excited about having a new baby around the house and hoping this time it is a boy because there are too many girls in this household already.

December 11, 1963, Mom has gone into labor and Mr. James rushed her to the hospital. After thirty minutes in the labor room, Mom gave birth to another girl. They named her Brenda and she looks so much like Mr. James that if she had been a boy his name would have been James Bower II. Sara came home to see the new baby and to meet the rest of us. She had not seen any of us who were born after Linda. We were hoping she could stay longer than two-weeks but she has to return to work. We had only seen pictures of her and we thought her, in the pictures, was the most beautiful person we have ever seen, but in person she was even more beautiful. She actually looks just like Mom. We are glad to get to see her and spend some time with her also.

Mr. James has asked Mom over and over again to marry him, with her continuously turning him down. I think because of all the hurt she had from the pass marriages that she is cautiously. Mr. Bower continuously asked her at least twice a month, even though she would decline the offer every time.

I'm ten years old now. Mom again is expecting to give birth to her tenth child. We again are hoping for a boy.

January twenty-eight, 1965, Mom is being rushed off to the hospital but this time the labor lasted a few hours before she delivered. After fourteen hours of hard labor Mom had given birth to another girl. Mom arrived home with our new baby sister after three days in the hospital. I held her for about thirty minutes and within that short time I had developed a special bond with her. It was much different from with the other babies. I cannot explain it and as she got older the bond got stronger. I would take her with me everywhere I went if it was possible and this helped Mom out a lot by giving her time for herself. I really enjoyed having Rachel with me. Sometime I had to remind myself that she was not my baby.

I'm twelve years old now and Dad reminds me that it is time for me to return home to Mom. I will come to Dad's house now on the weekend as I did with Mom. I was not ready to leave but know Dad is right about Mom could tell me things about how my body will change over the next year or so. I packed most of mine belongs but left enough there for my weekend visits.

I have been back with Mom for two years and finally settled in. Rachel and I have become even closer than before. People are beginning to believe that Rachel is my child with her being with me all the time. I would have had to given birth at the age of ten. I don't think so. I did not mind it so much what they thought because I looked at her as my baby anyway.

At fourteen, I got my first job. My first job was as a model for an Artist my Mom baby sat for. This was only for the summer while school was out. It gave me a chance to travel and save money. I planned to attend college after graduating from high school. During school sessions I would spend the weekends at Dad's house or in the privacy of my bedroom. When at home, I had Rachel to keeping me company, most of the time. Usually, after school Mr. James would be at our home preparing dinner for Mom. Mom needing time to rest from working two jobs and this was his way of giving her time to rest once she got home. Today he is here and preparing dinner but he had to leave to go to the store. Brenda, being mischievous as always, decided to sample dinner. In doing so, she dropped a piece of meat on the floor by the stove and left it there. Mr. James returned from the store, while in the kitchen he notices the meat on the floor. He asked: "Who was in the kitchen, in the pot?" No one answered. Meanwhile, I'm in my room studying. When he did not get an answer from the other children, he came to my bedroom door and because the door is lock; he kicked the door in. Asking me if I was the one who had been in the kitchen. I said "No, and you did not have to kick my door in to ask me that." His says: "If no one tells, I will spank everyone in the house, until someone tells who has been in the kitchen. Brenda never said one word. I said to him; 'You're not spanking, me.' He replies: 'If you are too grown to be spanked, leave.' I packed a few pieces of clothing and went to my Dad's house, telling him what had happen. Dad got very upset and called Mom. Mom is at work. Dad told her; 'You need to talk with James.' 'I do not want to have to handle it myself.' Mom asked Dad to bring me to her job. She reassured him that she would have a talk with Mr. James. Dad dropped me off at Mom's job and told me to call him tomorrow. Mom was standing in the door way waiting for me to arrive. When I entered the house, boy! , Did I get into trouble? She was angry because I should have called her first, instead of going to my Dad. When we got home, Mr. James was still there and I do not think he ever found out how the meat got on the floor. Mom asked Mr. James to join her in the kitchen to talk. I tried to listen in on the conversation but could not get close enough without being seen or heard. Mr. James obviously, got upset because of what Mom had to say. He stormed out of the house without saying another word.

A month later, Mr. James went out with a few of his friends and had a few too many drinks. Instead of going home as he usually did afterwards, he came to our house. He went into Mom's bedroom. I do not know to this day if he was horse playing or not, he had never done it before. I was asleep, when Al woke me by shaking me and saying: "May, Mr. James is pulling Mom from the bed by her foot. I jumped out of bed rubbing my eyes and headed toward Mom's bedroom, when I reached the door and could see that Mr. James was pulling Mom off the bed by her foot. I stepped into the room, asking: 'What the heck is going on in here?' Mom looked up at me as she pulled her leg away from him and at the same time, telling me: 'I'm all right, you can go back to bed.' I asked her: 'Are you sure, Mom?' She answered: 'I'm sure, he has been drinking but I can handle him.' 'You can go on back to bed.' I turned to go back to my bedroom, when I felt something cold against my back. Mr. James had reached up to a gun rack hanging over the top of Mom's bed and removed a rifle from it. Not knowing what it was, I reached for it. That is when I knew what it was. He had stuck the barrel of the rifle in my back. I became very angry and the only thing that ran through my mind was to protect me. I grabbed a vase from the top of the floor model television and with very little effort swinging it to hit Mr. James. The vase hit Mr. James on the side of his face and head. The impact was so powerful that Mr. James lost his balance falling backwards into the kitchen, landing on the floor by the back door. Still full of rage, I raised the vase a second time to hit him again, but Mom put her arm out to stop the blow. The vase hit Mom's wrist with such force that it broke her watch into tiny pieces and caused her wrist to bruise and swell. Mr. James lay there unconscious for a while but after about two hours he is conscious. Once he had gotten his head clear, he called the police. Sheriff Stan Johnson came to our home to take the report. When Sheriff Johnson heard what happened, he turned to Mr. James, saying; 'You are lucky.' 'Teenagers get really angry and protective of their Mothers if she gets threatened.' The next morning, Mr. James came to the house and entered the living room asking in a joking manner: 'Which one of you did this to me?' Mr. James is pointing to his swollen, bruised face and head. I just looked at him without saying a word. Mr. James then apologized to me for what happened last night. We now have developed a different kind of respect for each other. We even became friendlier with each other after a few months. In August, eight days before my fifteenth birthday Mr. James and Mom married.

Now that it is getting close for school to start, I'm leaving for Chicago, Illinois, to stay with my sister, Linda. I would be attending a high school that offers a program that would allow me to graduate two years earlier from high school, with a grade point average of 3.5 to 4.0.

I arrived in Chicago, two days before school starts. Once I settled in at Linda's home, she took me over to Kim's home to introduce me to her. Kim and I became very close and spent most of my spare time over at her house.

School has started, but I had to enroll in Stony Island High because the school, St. Bernard, I was to attend is full. I can take the courses that St. Bernard offered until space become availably for me there.

The two years passed quickly and I'm now attending St. Bernard. With one month left before I graduate, on my way to school I stopped in the lobby to check the mail. While standing here reading a letter from a friend in Texas, the janitor screamed: "Look at your leg." I brushed him off because he teased me before about how skinny my legs are. I thought that he maybe teasing me now, but with the expression on his face this time I thought I should take him seriously. I looked down at my leg and saw blood streaming down into my shoe from the lower part of my leg. When I saw the blood, my leg started to hurt very badly. I reached down grabbing my leg and could feel something hanging out of the exit wound. Apparently I got shot and had not felt a thing. The janitor ran into the Managers Office to call for an ambulance and the police. The ambulance never arrived, but the police arrived twenty minutes after the call. I could not believe I'm being taken to the hospital in the back of a police paddy wagon. Thank goodness there was no permanent damage to my leg, just a scar, to remind me of the unpleasant stay in Chicago. Linda called Mom and she thought that it was best that I return home. I did not want to leave until I finished school.

Before I left for the airport to return to Texas, Mom called telling me: "Do not tell your Dad anything about the shooting and leave the crutches on the plane. Your Dad would have a heart attack if he found out what happened to you." I agreed with her about not telling him. We could not stop him from meeting me at the airport and she also knew his habit of carrying me as if I'm still an infant. If by chance he did not carry me like he usually does, I will not be able to hide my injury, with the limp I have. He will for sure ask what is wrong and I could never lie to him.

I'm here in Texas at the Amarillo Airport and I have spotted Dad waiting. I stepped down on the last step from exiting the airplane, Dad reached and lifts me to carry me as usual. When Dad had reached the baggage claims, he put me down long enough to check on my luggage. My luggage was not on the plane. Dad will have to return for them or have them delivered to me later. Dad then reached and picked me up again, carrying me to the parking lot where he had a surprise waiting. Entering the parking lot, Dad raised his arm pointing in the direction of a brand new candy apple red Ford Mustang wrapped with a very large white bow. Dad is walking toward the car and at the same time, saying: 'Baby, this is your graduation gift.' 'I hope you like it.' I wrapped my arms around his neck giving him the tightest hug I could and kissed him on the cheek, saying: "Thank you, Dad. I love it very much. Thank you." He opened the car door placing me in the seat underneath the steering wheel. With all the excitement, I forgot about my leg. I started her up and drove to Mom's house with Dad following behind me. Dad came into the house, greeting Mom and Mr. James and to give Mom the papers on the car, for safekeeping. He did not stay long he just wanted to make sure I made it home safely.

After about two hours of observing Mom and Mr. James, I could see the same sparks in her eye from the day they got married. She is very happy even after taking her
"Five Times: The Best Was Last

CHAPTER ONE

Not knowing how much like my Mother I was,
That I would go through the same or similar things she had.

I'm hoping that I will be able to start where I left off with the relationship with Harvey Stone. We had dated for a year and had gotten engaged before I left to go to Chicago. We were able to continue the relationship but it did not last long because on his graduation last night he did not pick me up. The next day I spoke with his Mom and she too thought he had taken me. I found out later that day that he had taken someone else. It made me feel hurt, disappointed and angry. Lying across my bed in tears, I heard a knock at my bedroom door. I opened it, hoping it is Harvey to apologize. It was not Harvey instead is one of Al's co-worker and friend, Anthony Michaels, standing in my bedroom doorway. Anthony visited Al at our home daily but I never noticed him, until he was standing there in my bedroom doorway. He had heard me crying and wanted to try to cheer me up by asking me to join him, Al, and Sharon, who is his sister to Thompson Amusement Park. Saying it will make me feel better. I agreed to join them. We rode most of the rides at the park and ate all kinds of food. The conversation touched everything except the reason that I was so upset earlier. We were having a really good time and before we realized it, it was closing time for the park. Anthony drove me home and I thanked him for a really good time and also for helping me feel much better. I walked into the house asking Mom if Harvey had called. "He had not called." She answered. I decided at this very moment not to worry about Harvey anymore. I had such a good time with Anthony and I would not mind seeing him again.

Anthony and I begin dating. After two months, he left to help his Parents move to a different city.

Anthony left three weeks ago to help his parents move. On August 10 that happened to me my seventeenth birthday, Anthony called wishing me the best. He to my surprise, he asked me to marry him. I did not take him seriously at first and started to giggle. He did not think it was funny at all. Through his heavy bass voice, he snapped: 'I'm not joking.' I love you and would like for you to become my wife. 'Don't answer me now, I will call back in about two hours and you can give me your answer then.' After Anthony hung up the telephone, I dashed to the other side of the house to Mom's bedroom. Catching my breath and I began telling Mom what Anthony asked me on the telephone. Mom was just sitting there and she does not seem to be at all surprise. Mom says: 'I already knew about this because Anthony talked to me before he left about marrying you.' Saying; "It is your decision to make." I turned around to return to my bedroom, and shocked at the response I had gotten from Mom. I headed back to my room with my mouth wide open. I at least expected her to tell me I'm too young to be thinking about marriage or at least a lecture. I already know how my Dad will react to this news and did not look forward to telling him. He will have a cow. Picking up the telephone to call and when Dad answered, I begin with the usual small talk, then I told him. "Dad, I'm thinking about getting married." Like I thought, he had "two cows. With me being stubborn, he is not able to change my mind. I have always had my own mind and in doing so, I sometimes got into trouble. Now, Mom is giving me permission to have my own mind. 'This was a switch."

Two hours had passed when the telephone finally rang. I answered it and it was indeed Anthony and I told him "Yes" I will be his wife. He yelling back into the background and I heard him telling his parents; "Dad, she said yes." They had him to tell me 'welcomed' to the family and congratulation.

Anthony returned back to Amarillo on the twenty-eighth of September, bringing with him, his parents, brothers and sisters for the wedding. Glenda, his oldest sister lived here in Amarillo. I had made all the arrangements, except for picking up the tuxedos and our wedding rings. My Dad with reluctance agreed to be the one to give me away. Unfortunately his brother passed away the day before the wedding, so he had to leave town to attend the funeral. I asked Mr. James if he would substitute for my Dad to give me away. He said: "I will be very happy and proud to be the one to walk you down the isle." We have gotten to be very close.

Today is the 30th of September and the time has come, I'm so nerves, I cannot stop sweating. I hope everything will go according to plans, without any problems. I entered the doorway to the congregation and took a quick glance. I started to walk down the isle. I could feel my heart beating out of control. As I looked around, I could see many familiar faces; some were happy, some with excitement, but a lot filled with envy. I have looked forward to this day and I'm not about to let anyone or anything ruin my special day. I finally reached the front of the pulpit to stand next to the man I have chosen to spend the rest of my life with and my eyes started to fill with tears of joy. They were not tears of regret or from hesitation but these were tears from the reality that I will not just be Daddy's little girl, but I'm now also Anthony's wife. Anthony is standing there with the biggest smile on his face and I think he is trying his best to cover up just how nervous he really is. He took my hand, holding it tightly trying to gain some kind of control of his hand, which is now shaking out of control. Anthony looked into my eyes, smiling, but serious. The minister is saying: "We gathered here today to join Anthony and Ellen in Holy Matrimony." Finally the Minster reached the part that says: "You are now 'Husband and Wife' and you may now kiss your Bride." Anthony raised the veil over my face and head. Then he slowly moved in closer to place a gentle kiss on my lips. The kiss was passionate and had lasted longer than I thought, at least for a few seconds, then though the silence came a few, 'ooooooooooooooh, oooooooooooooooooh, oooooooooooooh's.' He came up for air and smiling out at the crowd of people that cheered him on. We both turned around facing the guest and family members, with each of them coming to kiss the bride and shaking the hand of the Groom to congratulate us. The entrance was thinning out and as I looked up I could see that Dad had returned back from his trip and was walking through the crowd of people toward us. Reaching his arms out as he got close enough to give me a hug. The closer he got, I could see tears rolling down his cheeks. He hugged me tightly and at same time lifting me from the floor. Dad placed me back on my feet and released me from his tight embrace, he than reached for Anthony's hand to greet him, pulling him in closer to him. When Dad had Anthony, up close enough he began to whisper, doing his usual, threatening anyone who would give me a second look, saying to Anthony: 'Don't you hurt my baby and you take good care of her and if you can't, bring her home just the way you got her?' 'Putting absolute fear in Anthony, You could see the fear in his eyes.'

Returning home from the reception, we arrived to the telephone ringing. It was Mrs. Stone, calling to let me know Harvey had tried to commit suicide, after hearing that I was getting married today. He will pull through the suicide attempt but not from me marrying someone else.

Three months into our marriage and everything is great, still in the honeymoon stage. I'm not feeling well and thinking I have a cold or the flu. I made an appointment to see the doctor and after a complete physical, he told me I did not have a cold or the flu, but I'm about eight weeks into my pregnancy. My first thought was, I hope Anthony would share the same excitement as I do. I do not know how he will feel about starting a family so soon because we only been married for a short time. It is a little too late to worry about that now.

I rushed home to prepare a special meal to celebrate. I'm hoping that it will be a celebration. It seems as though time is passed by slowly, but I know it is because of the anticipation and excitement.

It is 4:30 p.m., Anthony walks through the door and I ran to greet him, almost making him lose his balance. Giving him, a tight hug and a kiss made him suspicious. He asked: "What have you bought? It must have cost me a lot of money, with this kind of greeting." I answered: "I have not bought anything." Thinking: "What I'm about to tell you will cost you a lot of money in the long run." Saying: "Sit down because I have something to tell you." He sat down, with a confused look on his face. I sat on his lap with my arms around his neck, asking: "When do you want to start having children?" He replied: "When it happens I will be ready." Thrilled at his response, I blurted out: "Well, it has happened." I looked at his face to see what his expression would be. "You are going to be a Daddy. I went to the doctor today and he told me, I'm about eight weeks into my pregnancy already. He jumped up, almost knocking me to the floor, asking: 'Are you sure?' I answered: 'Yes, I'm sure,' He ran to the other room, picking up the telephone. I did not know how to take this reaction, whether he is happy or not. When he started talking, I then realized he was talking with his parents, I knew he is happy to know he will be a Daddy. He began telling his parents, saying: 'Guess what?' You are going to be Grandparents. "Ellen found out today that she is about eight weeks into her pregnancy." I assumed they were just as thrilled as I was if not more, this is their first grandchild. "Anthony's reaction let me know that he wants to become a Daddy."

Time went by fast, as we prepared for the arrival of our baby. Anthony waited on me, hand and foot, even carrying me when out in the snow.

It is getting close to the time for our baby to be born in about a month. Anthony got up this morning saying he is going to pick up a part for our car and he will be leaving about noon. When he left, I lay on the bed to take a nap but once I lay down I could not go to sleep but I had the sudden urge to walk to the store. By now Anthony has been gone two hours. I did not want anything in particular, just an urge to go to the store. The distance from our house could not be any more than six blocks. I dressed and started to walk to the store, taking a path I have never taken before. As I walked passed an apartment complex, I noticed a car parked there that was a lot like ours and the closer I got I could see that it was indeed our car. I did not know any reason for our car being parked there because I did not know anyone who lived there and did not think he knew anyone who lived there either. Puzzled, I turned around to return back home, without ever reaching the store.

It is now six p.m. I know it does not take six hours to pick up a part for a car. Especially after seeing our car parked at the apartment building made me wonder if he ever went to get a part for the car.

It is six twenty five p.m., when Anthony decided to walk through the back door after being gone for so many hours. He nor I did not say a word. Thinking: 'How can I bring up the subject without accusing him because I really did not have anything to accuse him of, but seeing the car parked at the apartments?' After a half hour of silence, I asked: "What would you do if you caught me with another man?" He looked up at me with a weird look on his face as if wondering what made me ask him this question. Anthony thought for a minute, then answered: "I will kill him." He asked: "What would you do if you caught me with another woman?" I answered: "I will leave you." He dropped his head and began to sob. I asked him: "What is wrong?" Anthony wiped his eyes with the back of his hand and blurted out: "I need to tell you something but I'm afraid." I knew then for sure he had been unfaithful. I said: "Don't be afraid, it can't be that bad." Pretending I did not have a clue to what he had done. Still never looking up at me, he said: 'I just did something and I knew better than to do it and it is eating me up inside.' 'What have you done?' "That is so bad, I asked." "I have been unfaithful to you, and I'm so sorry. There is no excuse for what I have done. I'm so sorry. I know this does not change the fact that I have been unfaithful but can you ever forgive me. Please, don't leave me. Please don't. I could not stand to lose you and my baby." I stood up, swinging my fist to hit him, but he grabbed my hand to stop me. "You should have thought about that before you jumped into someone else's bed.", I replied. I'm so angry I could feel my blood boiling in my veins. I pulled my hand away from him and went into the bedroom, slamming the door behind me. Anthony or I said anything for a while to each other. I returned back to the living room where he is still sitting with his head held down in shame and I asked one hundred and one question, demanding he answered them all. I wanted the complete details of what happened, minute by minute. He answered them all, hesitantly knowing it will only make me madder. Now I'm even angrier than before. I could not believe he did this to me. I insisted he sleeps on the couch. When morning came, I drove him to the health department for testing for venereal diseases and thank goodness he had not brought anything home. I still insisted he continues sleeping on the couch for the next month. I never told anyone that we were having problems in our marriage. I hoped that we could handle them ourselves. Anthony told me the woman was one of Glenda's co-workers and she had set him up with a date with her. Still this is no excuse for his actions and he should have been man enough to turn her down. By telling me this, put Glenda on my hate list.

Two days later, Glenda was knocking at our door. Her husband, Gus had beaten her. Ordinarily, I would have come to her aide but this time she is on her on after what she has done. With reluctance's, Anthony took her home, because she can no longer come to our house. He did not want any more trouble after what he has done. Gus, in the pass as well as now have continuously beat Glenda throughout their marriage, which caused them to not have children. Glenda stayed with him still.

A week before Sharon is born, Anthony and I decided to go shopping for a few more things for the baby. With the nursery being completed the only things I had to pick up being sleepers and blankets. When we reached the mall I entered Robert Hall's Department Store and Anthony went into the auto parts' store across the street from the mall. While I was in the children's department, I over heard a woman, who was standing in the doorway of the Robert Hall's store scream out: "He went that way." I walked over to the door, to see what was happening and my mouth dropped to the floor, when I saw that it was Anthony, being chased by the police and store security officers. I quickly walked across the street to where Anthony parked our car and by the time I made it cross the street, Anthony was in custody. The police had him hand cuffed and sitting in the back sit of the police car. I walked over to the Police Officer and told him who I was and asked if he could release Anthony's wallet and car keys to me. That is when the officer told me why they had Anthony under arrest for stealing. Anthony had stolen a package of race car stripes and when the store security officer confronted him he ran from the store. The officer had already taken Anthony's wallet from his pocket and had seen all the money he has in it. The officer asked Anthony why he had done such a foolish thing. Anthony did not answer but held his head down in shame. The officer than gave his things to me, as he shook his head in disguised. After the police officers hand me Anthony's wallet, I then found a pay phone. I called my Mom and Mr. James to come pick me up because I'm too large to fit behind the steering wheel to drive myself home. When they arrived, Mom asked me if I was going with them to the courthouse to see if Anthony will receive fines and released. I answered: "No, and I hope they keep him locked up for life." I opened his wallet to show them the hundred dollars' bills in it and that there is no reason for Anthony to do such a thing. Mom nor Mr. James said a word but I could see the disappointment in their eyes but still Mom was not to let him stay in jail, if she had anything to do with it. After being released, Mom and Mr. James brought him home.

Anthony walked into the house but Mom and Mr. James did not come in, knowing how angry I am and also knowing it will be trouble once Anthony walked through the door. I did not say anything to him but the look on my face said it all. He really did not want to know what I'm thinking about him at this moment.

On May 24, 1973, our daughter was born. We named her after his sister, Sharon Ann, weighing 7 lb. 1/2 oz and at three weeks old, the doctors diagnosed her as a chronic asthmatic. I spent many days and nights in the hospital with her, having very little support from Anthony.

While trying to get our marriage back on track and take care of our new baby my hands are full. We moved into a large home shortly after I found out I'm pregnant with our second child.

I thought everything is great with our marriage but found out Anthony decides to have another affair and again he got caught. This time he got caught by my Mother and that scene really got ugly. Mom was very fond of Anthony, she thought he could do no wrong, but now he has tarnished that image for good. The way I am feeling now has left a very bitter taste in my mouth. I did not like the way I felt, because living with Anthony now difficultly. I stayed only to save money to prepare to leave him. David Joe was born June 17, 1974, weighing 7 lb. 4 1/2 oz and we have two children and again needed even more living space. We moved into this house five months ago and again I'm pregnant with our third child. This time the doctor diagnosed me positive for toxemia. By the time I made it to the doctor's, not knowing I was pregnant, I'm already twenty-five weeks into the pregnancy. The doctor says the reason I did not show any signs and my baby was not moving like she should be because of the toxemia in my system. The doctor is suggesting, I not carry the baby any longer and if I tried to we would be in danger. He went as far as giving the baby and me a 50/50 chance to even survive the birth. I replied: "I have carried my baby this far and I'm not going to let you take her now." I insisted he not tells Anthony or my Mother about the risk I'm taking to have my baby. The doctor will be watching me closely for the remaining three months.

Three weeks before, our baby is due, Anthony has surgery to remove kidney stones. During his hospital stay I found out that he was also having another affair. This time it is one of his co-workers and she showed up at the hospital to see him. I'm sure she had not planned to be there when I arrived, but I arrived before she had a chance to leave. I arrived early enough to see her leaving his hospital room as I approached it. She walked right pass me as I headed to the entrance to his room and when I entered I asked him: "Whom was that woman just leaving your room?" He lied as usual. Anthony staggered his words, saying: "Shhheeee has thhhe wrrongggggge room." There is a sweet potato pie on his night table. I grabbed the pie, assuming she had brought it and left the room in enough time to catch her as she entered the elevator. I throw the pie, hitting her on the side of her head. Bulls Eye! 'Right on target' I stood there hoping she would say or make a move, so I will have a reason to beat her down. She did not even break her stride and she just got on the elevator as she wiped the pie off the side of her head and face with the back of her hand. She never stopped to look around. I returned to Anthony's room, walked over to the side of his bed. I raised my hand as high as I could and with as much force as I could. I hit Anthony in the very same spot that he had surgery at. He jumped and screamed so that as I'm walking from his room, heading to the elevators, the nurses ran by me, going to see what is wrong with him. I do not know what he told them and I really couldn't care less. I now know what the bitter taste in my mouth is, 'HATE.' I decided then I was not going back to the hospital again to see him.

Anthony is home from the hospital but our relationship is dying slowly, but surely. While he was still in the hospital, I had time to think about all he has put me through. I have decided to leave him when I have my baby and well enough to travel.

Two weeks later, Cherry is born, August 5, 1975. She weighed 7 lbs. 14 1/2 oz and even with the problems I had she appeared to be healthy. With all the hard work during labor I had no energy left it being drained completely. In seven days I will leave the hospital and go home.

I have just arrived home from the hospital and still planning to leave when the baby and I are able to travel. After telling Anthony of my plans, he is not happy about them at all and begged me not to leave. He is now suggesting we all move to Minneapolis, for a new start. He said he would go first. I cannot believe I'm listening to this, knowing he will be back to his same tricks but I agreed still. He says: "I will stay with your sister, Barb until I find work and a place for us to live."

Anthony has been in Minneapolis for a month. He called to tell me he found a job and a place for us to live. He would be sending for us in two weeks.

We are here in Minneapolis and in our own apartment for three months and I have started working now too. I worked nights, while Anthony is home with the children.

It is now January 1976, cold and snowing and I'm at work, when I received an emergency call. It is not Anthony but the call is about him. It is the Police calling me and the first thing to come out of my mouth is: "Are my children all right?" The officer quickly answered: "Ma'am, your children are fine but your husband, on the other hand, has been placed under arrest and we need you to come home." After the officer finishing telling me the details of what happened I did not say a word, hanging up the telephone and ran to get my coat to leave. On the route home I thought about what the officer told me on the telephone. Saying: 'Anthony, left the children unattended in the apartment, while he is out side stealing a battery from someone's car and the fire alarm went off in the building.' When the landlord opened the apartment, she found your children alone and crying inside. 'The landlord than called us, not knowing that the person whom we have arrested already was the Father of the children.' They told me because Anthony left the children alone they charged him with child endangerment and theft of private property for taking the battery. I arrived home to my apartment filled with police officers. Two officers are in the kitchen talking with Anthony. I started walking toward the kitchen where Anthony was sitting when one of the officers stopped me, saying: "You are too angry and I cannot allow you near him until you have settled down." The officer talked with me until he was sure I had calmed down, then all of the officers left, not taking Anthony with them. I did not want to even look at Anthony's face or talk with him fears of doing something I will regret. I put my babies back to sleep, then went into the bedroom to get a blanket to cover myself while I slept on the couch because I did not want to be any-where near him.

It is morning and I'm still not speaking to Anthony as he prepares for work. I'm waiting anxiously for him to get in the car to drive off. I could not sleep for thinking about how I was going to leave him. When he drove off, I started to pack the children and my clothes, then called my brother-in-law, Jesse, to take us to the airport. Jesse is hesitant, not wanting to get involved in our problems but I was finally able to convince him to take us to the airport. The children and I are on our way back to Texas.

Anthony arrived in Amarillo a week after the children and I had and had decided to go into the Air Force, mainly to keep from telling his parents the real reasons we are sep-arating. I have moved in with my Mother and stepfather. Anthony and I agreed to take this time while he is in Boot Camp, to make sure if I really wanted to end our marriage.

After boot camp, Anthony transferred to Biloxi for six months and then to Keesler Air Force for his training. The children and I came to Moss Pointe, Mississippi to stay with my Aunt Amy in order to be near Anthony. Moss Point is only ten miles from Biloxi that is close enough for us to spend the weekends together.

Anthony had successfully finished his training and has received his orders to report to Scott Air Force Base in Illinois. He says that Sharon, Cherry and I will have to return to Amarillo until his is able to get a place for us to live and we will join him then. I did not believe anything Anthony says because he has lied so many times. So again the children and I are heading back to Amarillo. Not knowing the reason for him wanting to be at Scott Air Force Base was to be near a woman he met there.

My children and I arrived in Amarillo and after being in Amarillo for about a week I had gotten a job working for Wesley Community Center. This will keep me busy, while Anthony is looking for a place for us to live, thinking to myself.

The children and I have been in Amarillo now for eight months. Anthony had plenty of time to find a place for us to live, but every time he calls I heard the same old thing from him: "I still have not found a place yet." Over and over, week after week, we would hear this from him. The children don't remember their Father's face any longer and I have gotten really tired of being alone. I decided that when he calls again, the first thing that comes out of my mouth will be, "we come either now or not at all." He called and when I told him this. He says right away: "I will check to see if there is Base Housing available." Anthony has not checked when there should have been the first place to check for housing, thinking to myself. When he called back, of course now he says there is housing and he now has a place for us. I'm angrier even more because he should have checked Base Housing first and he may have, just want this time to do whatever he wanted. Sharon, Cherry and I will be leaving for Scott Air Force Base in two days.

We are here at Scott Air Force Base and he does not seem to be very happy to have us here. A few days have passed and I still feel as if I have interrupted his life. What is it, I'm not sure, but I'm sure he did not prefer that we be here?

After being here for two weeks, I thought it would be nice to surprise Anthony for lunch. I took the children to the Base nursery and went to the Mess Hall. When I walked up to the door to look for Anthony, I found him sitting at a table with a woman. They are holding hands underneath the table. It is like they are hiding what they are doing from the other people inside the Mess Hall. I started to go in and strike out at him but caught myself, thinking: "Why create a scene with him because you just keep setting yourself up to be hurt over and over? I was the one who got surprised." I turned around and walked out. Thinking to myself, now I know why he was so distance from me when I arrived at the Base because of being involved with someone else. I'm angry because he could have just told us to stay in Texas, instead of having me come here to the mess, again. This time I have had enough. I picked my children up from the nursery and driving home in deep thoughts, thinking: 'I will take a trip to Minneapolis alone and check out things, for preparation to move back there.' If everything works out O.K., I will return to get my children and come back to Minneapolis, permanently. I got my children out of the car and we entered the house. I feed them lunch and put them down for a nap when they finished. I packed two suitcases for my trip to Minneapolis and set them aside. I then sat on the sofa to watch television but my mind wondered went to what I had seen earlier. My thoughts got interrupted when I heard the car drive up. Did not realized time have passed so quickly because I was in such deep thoughts, since I arrive home? Anthony is walking in the door as if he has done nothing. Sharon, DJ, and Cherry are awake now too. He was smiling and playing with the children. I'm sitting quietly, watching him, wondering how does he think, he can get away with this. Well, I guess he thinks he has gotten away with it.

I watched Anthony and the children playing around for a few and then went to prepare dinner.

I have set the table for dinner and called everyone into the dinning room. No one is saying a word, the children are quiet, as if they know something is wrong. Everyone finished their dinner but I did not have much of an appetite. When everyone finished their dinner, I cleaned the kitchen and then gave the children their baths. I read them two bedtime stories and putting them to bed afterwards. It is now time to sit down to talk with Anthony. Trying not to show my anger by calming myself down, I began telling him of my plans to take an overdue vacation but never mentioning anything about what I had seen earlier. I did not ask him but insisted that he take the time off to take care of his children. I need this well-deserved vacation to eliminate stress and a break from everything else. I was not taking "No" for an answer. I told Anthony I will be staying with Carolyn while I'm in Minneapolis.

Carolyn is going through similar problems. Her husband has been cheating on her for the pass two years and has separated now. Their children are having a hard time with what has happened and their relationship with their Father will never be the same again. I do not think the family will be able to recover from this.

I arrived in Minneapolis. Minnesota on Saturday at six thirty p.m. on January 1978 and Carolyn is waiting at the gate for me. I spoke with Carolyn before I left for the airport in Illinois. Carolyn has made plans for us to go out tonight. I told her: "Great, I would like very much to go out on the town and maybe I will be lucky to meet someone nice for a change." Describing to her, the man, I would like to meet, telling her: "I want him to be tall, light complexion, nice hair and handsome. We arrived at her home and I went in, headed straight for the bathroom to take a bath and freshened up for a night on the town. As I walked from the bathroom, I heard someone knocking at her door. It was a young man from her church stopping by. I think my sister is trying to play matchmaker. I looked down stairs to see who it was. If she is trying to match the description I gave her, she is way off base. The only part of the description he has is the complexion. My niece met me on the stairs teasing: 'Your date is here.' She started to laugh uncontrollable. Without thinking, I said aloud: 'He is not my date.' I think he heard me because he left without saying a word. Carolyn and I finished getting dress. We are now heading to several night clubs: the Hippogriff, Naucurema and the Tempo will be the last stop tonight. It is getting late and I still have not seen anyone close to the description I wanted. I looked around the club and not until I looked on the dance floor, did I spot the man of my dreams. Having every last one of the traits, I have described to Carolyn. Boy, did he look good. So good, I could not keep my eyes off him. I just throw discrepancy out the door. I could not help myself. Finally he caught me starring and I could not even turn my head or close my eyes. My eyes would not move from him. Carolyn wanted to know what I was starring at so hard. When she turned her head in the direction I'm looking and she caught the same view I had. She then replied: 'There he is, the man you described to me.' I looked away from him just long enough to say to Carolyn: 'He will come over here.' Like I was so sure of myself he would. Just when I turned my head to find him again, he appeared standing right over our heads. My heart skipped three beats, when I saw him standing there. He leans over to say something to Carolyn. I felt embarrassed and disappointed, thinking he was asking Carolyn to dance with him. He was asking her: 'Can I put my coat on the back of your chair?' After he had placed it there, he leans over again, asking her: "Is it OK for me to dance with your sister? She answered: 'Yes, if she wants to dance with you?.' Knowing, I want nothing more than to dance with this gorgeous man. He held his hand out to take mine, helping me from the chair. He is leading me to the dance floor and I'm in heaven and did not have to die to get there. Looking up at him, standing there, dressed in dark green tuxedo and every bit of six feet three inches, as if he has just stepped out of the GQ magazine. With big dark eyes, soft dark brown hair with large locks of curls hanging down passes his shoulder, and built better than Fort Knox. He is dancing with me, only me, song after song. I closed my eyes and was afraid to open them, thinking he will disappear or I was only dreaming but when I opened my eyes he was still there. The club is only thirty minutes from closing and the song has ended. We walked back to the table where Carolyn is still waiting. He pulled my chair out for me to sit down and as he pushed my chair in closer to the table, he began to introduce himself to us, saying: "My name is Sean Mays." Carolyn and I said hello and introduced us to him. Sean, asking Carolyn, if he could take me with him to an after hour party, as if I was not even standing here. I guess this is his way to win her confidence. Promising to bring me home safe, as he is writing down his name, address and telephone number to reassure her. Carolyn says: 'She is a grown woman and does not need my permission to go with you.' 'You need to ask her if she wants to go with you.' With a warm smile Sean turned to me and apologizes for not asking I first. Then he asked me if he could have the pleasure of my company in joining him to an after hour party. I answered "Yes, I will join you, if you promise I will be safe." We then left the club and walked Carolyn to her car. Carolyn asked for me to call to let her know when I will be arriving home. Sean and I left and drove to the after hour party. When we arrived at the party and being there for a few minutes I did not feel comfortable, so Sean and I left. We rode until we reached Logan Street and I still do not have a clue to where we are or to where he is taking me. He soon pulled the car up into an alley way then into a drive way behind a large house with two floors and we got out of the car to enter through a back door. Sean turned to me saying: 'This is where I live, with my Mom.' I hope you do not mind me bringing you here. I promise we will not stay too long. You are safe.' I'm thinking, what could be his motive for bringing me here. After we reached the door, Sean reached into his pocket for his keys and realized he has lost them. He turned to me saying: 'I have misplaced my keys and when I wake up my Mom, she will not be very pleasant.' 'You will have to excuse her when she comes to open the door.' He begins knocking very hard on the door and after several knocks, his Mother opens the door. She was not at all what I expected. I expected to see an older gray hair and a little over weight person, instead appeared a very attractive and young look-ing middle age woman who could have passed for his sister. She opened the door and giving Sean a look to let him know she did not appreciate him waking her up. I guess she did not want to embarrass him with me standing there. Sean says: 'Mom, I lost my keys and I'm sorry I had to wake you.' She replied: 'Just don't let it happen again.' She turned around heading back to her bedroom. We entered and walked in behind her until she reached her bedroom and disappeared. Sean and I entered the living room. Sean told me to make myself comfortable and he disappeared into another room. He reappeared carrying in his arm a small child. The child must be at least twelve to eighteen months old. I'm assuming this is his son. Sean walks toward me, saying: 'This is my son, Keith.' Sean placed him on my lap. He is a very handsome child, looks a lot like Sean. After an hour, I told Sean it was getting very late and I should call Carolyn to let her know I will be home shortly. He replied: "I'm sorry. I have enjoyed your company so much. I do not want the night to end, but you are right it is late. I'm sure your sister is waiting up for you." Sean took Keith back to the bedroom and returned to help me with my coat. We went back through the house the same way we entered it and Sean locked the door, using his Mother's keys. When we approached the car Sean opened my door, standing there waiting for me to get in, so he could close the door. He went to the driver's side, getting in and began to drive me to Carolyn's house. We pulled up in front of the house and it is dark though out. Carolyn did leave the porch light on and the door unlocked. Sean got out of the car to open my door and while helping me out, he asked if I would give him a call before noon today. He walked me to the door, asking me again to call him before noon, but I really did not want to leave his side. I told him I would give him a call. Sean leans toward me, kissing me gently on the cheek before I went into the house. Before I closed the door, I said: "Good night." I entered the house, quietly and I went to the bathroom to take a shower. I put on my pajamas and lay on the couch. I wide awake and not feeling tired at all. I'm too excited about seeing this gorgeous man again.

The morning light starts shining sooner than I expected since I had stayed out so late. Everyone else is up getting ready for church. I only had about three hours sleep because I could not sleep for thinking about what will be the appropriate time to call Sean. I'm not letting him think I'm over anxious to call him. So, I have decided to call him, much later. I'm taking a chance of missing him all together. Everyone has left now and I'm here alone. Thinking if I'm doing the right thing by waiting to call Sean.

It is already two o'clock and Carolyn has arrived home from church with her children. Carolyn and I sat in the kitchen at the table, talking about last night, when I finally looked at the clock it was seven thirty p.m. I did not realized time had past so quickly. Thinking Sean for sure has gone home by now but I will call anyway. I'm thinking that I may have messed this up. I called and surprised that it was Sean's voice on the telephone. I quickly apologize to him for calling him so late. He said: 'After you did not call by noon, I decided to fill in for a co-worker who could not get here until later.' 'I was hoping you would call before he arrived.'

His asked: "Would you have dinner with me? I was hoping to spend the afternoon with you." I replied: 'Let me check with Carolyn to see if she had planned anything for tonight.' I pretended to ask Carolyn, by covering up the receiver for a few seconds. After a few seconds I removed my hand from the receiver and then answered: 'We do not have any plans for tonight, so yes I'm free for dinner.' He said; "I will pick you up in thirty minutes. Will this be enough time?" I answered: "Yes and hung up the telephone. I jumped up from the sofa to go take a quick shower and begin dressing. When I had finished the last touches to my hair, I heard a knock at the door. Looking out of the window to see Sean standing there, he did say thirty minutes and it has been exactly thirty minutes. I opened the door to greet him and at the same time reaching for my coat. He helped me with my coat, than we locked the door to the house. Pulling my coat closer to my shin because the wind is so cold, Sean and I walked to the car. After we were safely buckled in ours, seat belts, he started the car and began to drive. Sean drove a long way before we reached our destination, Rudolph's restaurant. I ordered The Boggy Dinner and Sean ordered The Valentino Dinner with them both being excellent, when we finished and headed to his home. He wanted to introduce me to the rest of his family. Sean's sister, Niki, a younger brother Don, Charles who is Dee's boy friend, Alberto a family friend and Neka his niece, Niki's daughter. Sean's Mother is still at work. We sat and talked for hours. It has gotten very late and Sean says he needed to run an errand and that he will be right back. Twenty minutes had passed, when Sean returned. I was looking out of the window as he approached the door and noticing him carrying luggage. The closer he got to the door entrance I could see that the luggage was mine. I asked him: 'What are you doing with my luggage?' With a big grin on his face, he said: 'You will be here for only two weeks and I want to spend every minute of it with you that's possible.' I very quickly replied; 'It is flattering that you would like to spend the two weeks with me but you just met me and know nothing about me.' I could not understand, what did he say to Carolyn to convince her to let him take my luggage without my consent? He answered: 'I like what I see and this way by the time you have to leave, we will know all we need to know about each other.' I explained: 'I have three small children and a husband.' Even though I have planned to leave him when I return home, I don't think I'm ready to jump into another relationship.

The two weeks passed quickly. Sean was correct because we did get to know each other better. I called home every other day to talk with my children. I miss them very much and was anxious to see them. I feel really close to Sean and I knew my children will like him too. For some reason, I trust him or was it that I wanted to trust him. Now it is time for me to leave Minneapolis and return home to my children and deal with Anthony. Sean drove me to the airport. As we are hugging and saying our good byes Sean released me long enough to reach into his pocket. Sean then hands me some money and at the same time saying: 'Take this money, go get your children and return to me.' 'If I do not hear something from you in forty-eight hours, I will come and get you.' I was speechless and shocked, not realizing he felt so strongly about me. I never told him I have planned to move to Minneapolis. I leaned over placing a kiss on his lips and telling him I will see you in two days. As I walked through the walk way to enter the plane, I stopped suddenly to wave bye and I blew kisses to him.

I arrived to Scott Air Force Base at six p.m. Anthony alone with the children is here to meet me. I'm not at all please to see Anthony's face, but thrilled to see my children, as they are to see me. The children ran to me almost knocking me down, covering me with big hugs and lots of kisses.

After arriving home and unpacking, I spent most of the evening with my babies, playing, feeding and giving them baths. Once the children were asleep, it was now time to deal with their Father. Asking him to sit in the living room with me so we could talk. I then told Anthony, saying; 'Anthony, the children and I will leave in two days going to Minneapolis to live.' I never mentioned Sean, knowing it could make him angrier and the situation would get ugly. Anthony surprised me. I thought he would be glad for me to leave but he seemed upset and was trying to convince me the whole time to change my mind. I made up my mind. After we finished talking, I started to pack the children and my clothes. Anthony paced the floor, periodically sticking is head in the door way of what use to be our bedroom, still trying to convince me to stay by promising to treat us better than he had. I know from experiences that his promises could not hold water. I ignored him so that he knew the conversation has ended. He eventually realized I paid him no attention and went back to the living room and I continued to pack. I went into the bathroom to take a long hot bath to relax. Now in my flannel pajamas, I lay on the couch, leaving Anthony in the bedroom where I soon fell asleep, but was woken by feeling my body being lifted from the couch. Anthony, as he is lifting me, saying: 'You are going to make love to me before you leave this house even if I have to take it.' I began to fight and struggling to get away from him and at the same time saying to him: "If you try to force me, I will kill you if I have to. You better put me down right now." I managed to get away from him. I ran into the kitchen to get the hammer, not knowing what he will try next. He did not dare follow me into the kitchen. I was finally able to get dress quickly, before lying back down on the couch. This time with the hammer in my hand, I'm still afraid to go back to sleep. I lay there on the couch with the hammer in my hand waiting in case I have to defend myself. The children slept through the scuffling with Anthony and I'm thankful for that. He did not bother me again.

Finally, it is time to go to the airport and I'm too ready to get away from this nightmare of a marriage before something bad happens. Our flight is leaving at nine o'clock A.M. and we will arrive in Minneapolis by eleven thirty A.M.

Upon arrival, Sean is standing there waiting at the gate to greet us. After reaching him and giving him a hug, he notices the bruises on my arm. Asking: "Where did you get the bruises from?" After I explained to him how I got them, he became very angry. Sean is angry enough to want to take the next flight back to Illinois to confront Anthony. I was finally able to calm Sean down with the help from my children and headed to the car. They seem to like him and he seems quit taken by them. This will make the move much easier. I still have some unfinished business with their Father, a divorce.

We arrived at Sean's house and we are settling in. I sat down with Sean to tell him what my plans were. The children and I are not planning to live here with him and his family, indefinitely. I do not plan to stay very long and will be looking for an apartment, starting tomorrow. Sean isn't thrilled with the ideal, calling his Mom to the room, hoping she will convince me, that we are welcome to stay. She was very convincing, but the children as well as I need our own place. I do not want Sean to think that he is responsible for us. He's intention is not to let us out to his sight.

Anthony called often, once he got the telephone number. Still

Anthony tried to get me to come back home. This is how he found out the children and I was living with Sean. Anthony became very bitter and finally filed for a divorce. He used the divorce to get back at me by asking for custody of our son. He lied to his attorney because telling his attorney he did not know where we were, I would not be able to receive the summons for court. If I did not appear in court, he can obtain custody of our son by default.

Two months after receiving the final divorce decree Anthony showed up at my door with the Sheriff and the court order granting him custody of David. Taking my son away, was the only way he could hurt me. The hate I have for him, I thought could not get any stronger, but I was wrong.

Sean and I drove to Scott Air Force Base to visit with DJ the following summer and pick up my car that I had left behind. Anthony is dating someone now by the name of, Brittany. She is also in the Air Force. Sean and I visited for three days. It was very hard to leave my son behind. I miss DJ so much and he have grown so much. I even considered taking DJ and running with him. I would not have gotten very far. Anthony would have liked nothing better than to have me arrested, if just to get even with me for leaving him. I will not give him the satisfaction. Convincing myself when DJ got older he will come to live with me and he will resent his Father for taking him from his sisters and me.

CHAPTER TWO

Door number one opened and is closing fast, so
Prepare for the opening of door number two.

It is March of 1979, the nineteenth to be exact. Sean and I
have been together now for a year and a very pleasant year at
that. At nine A.M., Sean called me from his Grandmother's
house and asked me to get dress. Telling me, his Aunt Fannie
wants us to ride to Watertown, South Dakota with her to
pick up some documents from the courthouse there. I
dressed and they picked me up at ten thirty A.M. Sean drives
for a few hours but it seems like days. We finally arrived in
Watertown, in front of the court house at three thirty p.m.
Sean leaves the car to enter the courthouse but his Aunt
never moved from the car. Thinking maybe he went to see if
we were at the right building. He returned to the car with a
clown grin on his face. We drove off and Sean never men-
tions anything about what happened in the courthouse.
Sean pulled up in front of a small building, which looked
like a wedding chapel. After parking the car, Sean walked to
the entrance and disappeared inside. After about five minutes he stuck his head out of the door, beckons for us to

come inside. We entered the chapel and I found myself standing in front of a minister. Sean took my hand and with a gentle voice he says: "Will you marry me? Will you be my wife, right now?" I froze for a few seconds allowing myself to come back down to Earth. I said: "What? What? He repeated: 'Will you be my wife?' In a state of shock, but yet conscious, I said: 'Yes, I will be your wife.' He leans forward, kissing me on the lips. I'm still in disbelief and cannot believe this is really happening to me. The ceremony is quick and to the point but it still had the same impact as a large wedding to me. Sean took my hand and we headed back to the car after the ceremony. I still cannot believe what had just happened. Thinking: 'Sean had to be really sure that I would not turn him down, to make this trip.' We drove back to Minneapolis. On the way back, I asked: 'When did you plan this?' 'Sean, why didn't you just ask me to marry you.' 'Sean you took a really big chance driving me all the way here and ask me to marry you.' I had no ideal you wanted to marry me. 'You never mention marriage to me.' He said with the biggest smile on his face: 'I plan to marry you the first time I met you, I knew you were the one.' We arrived home at eight p.m. The entire family is here to congratulate us. Sean's family decorated the house for the wedding reception. They all were in on this plot.

The next morning we are getting ready to go to the City Hall to get my name changed on my driver's license and social security card. Sean pulls his drivers' license but forgets he has lied to me about his age, to show me the picture on it. I looked at his license and shocked again. Sean told me the night we met, he was twenty four years old, but according to his drivers license he was only nineteen years old at the time. I was twenty two years old when we met. I guess it is a little too late to fuss about it now because I married him already. Sean looked at me smiling, realizing now I know he lied about his age. He could not say anything he just stood there smiling.

After two years, Sean is getting restless and started to run with the wrong crowd. I have tired to convince him this is not a good thing to do and I was afraid he would get himself into trouble. I argued with Sean many times but still I failed to get him to see that his actions were ruining our marriage. So I decided to leave. I did not want my children exposed to these bad influences. He though I was trying to run his life by trying to pick his friends, when I'm trying to save him from destroying our marriage and a possible run in with the law. I could not take it anymore. I have decided to move back to Texas, for two reasons. (1) I'm home sick, missing my parents and (2) I wanted to get my children from the bad environment, as well as myself. After I told him of my decision, he decided that he would come alone too. A week later we packed the car and before long we were in Texas. We lived with my Mother until we found jobs and our own apartment.

It is the summer of 1979 in August and we have been in our apartment for a month. Sean and I have planned to go out to celebrate my birthday and moving into our apartment. I walked through the door after work to find Sean has made it home already, which was strange. He never beat me home before, so right away, I thought he had become ill and his employer had let him come home early. I asked: "Are you sick?" He answered: "No, I'm not sick." When he would not go into details, I asked: "Why are you home so early?" He just sat there as if nothing else needs explaining. I'm still waiting for him to go into details about why he is home so early. So I asked again: "Why are you home so early?" Sean hesitated to answer me. I asked again: 'What happened?' He hesitated a few seconds before he replied: "I quite." I asked him, why because he refused to volunteer any more information. He answered: "They asked me to do something that is not in my job description." I interrupted him and asked: "What?" Just wanted to know what kind of explanation he had for walking off a good paying job. Whatever reason he had could not be shorter than risking his life, would be good enough for him too quite. He replied: "They asked me to sweep up broken glass." I'm now speechless from his reply and angry enough to scream. Instead, I told my children to go get into the car. 'So out done, I walked out the door without saying another word to him and took the children over to my Mother's apartment, while I alone to celebrate.' I walked the children up the stairs into Mom's apartment. Mom did not see Sean with me asked right away where Sean was. I did not want to go into details with her, so I just told her that he was at home. Mom did not ask me any more question. She could see the expression on my face and know something is wrong. I left Mom's and drove to the other side of town, to a club that my Dad visited often. I entered the doorway and stopped to see if I could spot Dad. Dad is sitting with some of his friends at a table. I walked over to the table to where they are and joined them. Within a few minutes I had forgotten about the trouble I'm having with Sean and I'm enjoying myself.

Now it is getting time to call it a night and I began telling Dad what is going on between Sean and me. Hoping he would follow me home, not knowing how angry Sean still is. Dad said he would follow me home, just in case Sean gets out of hand. We left the club and drove to my apartment. I arrived home, slowly walking up the stairs, allowing Dad enough time to park his car. Opening the front door, my first step in the doorway, I'm stepping on a pile of clothes and they are mine. Sean has thrown them throughout the apartment floor. I followed the trail of clothing to our bedroom and picking up a few of the pieces. The few pieces I picked up, Sean had taken scissors and cuts the clothing into pieces. I walked into the bedroom and Sean jumped to his feet walking toward me. Before he could reach me, there is a knock at the door. Dad entered the apartment, stepping onto the same piles of clothing. He knew things were about to get heated up before he entered the apartment. He walked passed me to the bedroom where Sean is, saying: "Don't you ever put your hand on her or you will be back in Minnesota sooner than you planned, in a pine box?" Sean looking innocent, he replied: "Mr. Rich, I did not put my hands on your daughter, asks her." Dad turned to me, asking: "Are you all right?" I told him that I'm fine. Dad turned around to leave. Sean disappeared in the bedroom and closed the door behind him. I went into one of the children's rooms to sleep.

The next morning, I woke to Sean standing over me and he began to apologize for what he did last night, but before he could finish, there is a knock at the door. I went to open the door and there stood my half sister, Loretta. She walked right pass me to where Sean is standing. The closer she got to Sean, she quickly put her hand inside of her pocket and pulled out the 38 magnums. She raised it high, sticking it into Sean's mouth and at the same time, saying: "Don't you ever think about putting your hand on my baby sister? I will blow your head off." Sean did not move a muscle except for the tears that started to flow down his cheeks, but he never said a word. He would have a hard time trying to say anything with the gun stuck in his mouth. Loretta turned toward me, asking: "Did he hit you?" The gun is still in Sean's mouth as she is talking to me I quickly answered: "No, he did not hit me." So she would remove the gun from his mouth. She finally put the gun back into her pocket, as she is saying to me: "If you need me, just call and I will be here in no time."

A few weeks passed and Sean or I never discussed what had happened again. He never did anything close to that again.

The weekend is finally here and the children are looking forward to us taking them riding, out to eat or to the Amusement Park. We all dressed and headed out to the car. We had decided to take a drive around the North Heights Park. North Heights Park is one of the most popular places for people of all ages to socialize. We drove around the park the first time and I heard someone say: 'Hey!' Ellen, baby I looked around to see if I could locate from where it came and who is calling out my name. I could see Lou Morgan standing close by. I than realized that it is Lou shouting out my name. 'When I lived in Amarillo a few years ago, he tried to talk to me, but I turned him down by telling him, he was too young.' Somehow he found out Sean is the same age he is and now he is angry. Sean drove around the park a second time. Again, I heard: 'Hey!' 'Ellen, baby' I am hoping Sean has not heard him but I was wrong he did hear it. Looking at the expression on Sean's face, I knew he was getting angry. He started to drive around again. I'm trying to convince him to take us somewhere else. He just ignored me and still heading to the same spot where we heard Lou call out my name. When Sean reached the very same spot, we heard it again: 'Hey!' 'Ellen, baby' This time Sean stops and gets out of the car. He ran to the back of the car to the trunk. Not sure of what he is planning to do, and I jumped out to stop him. Still asking him to take us somewhere else but Sean is not listening to me. Before Sean could get to the trunk, Lou had made it to a car parked not far from where he stood and retrieved a gun. I heard two or three loud booms when I realized Lou is shooting at us and by the time I reached to where Sean is standing with the trunk opened, Lou shoots several times more. One of the bullets hit the passenger side back tire, one hit the tail end of the car, one hit inside the trunk and the forth one hit Sean. I could see blood on Sean's shirt but did not know where Lou shot him. I looked over Sean's body for the location of the wound. Lou walks up behind Sean hitting him on the top of his head with the butt of the pistol. Lou ran quickly to a waiting car and fled. Sean still not knowing where the blood is coming from him, jumped into our car following the car that Lou had gotten into. I'm yelling for him to go to the hospital. The car tires flatten and Sean could not continue the chase. The tire slowly deflating, Sean drives slowly to the hospital's emergency room. Lou shot Sean in the upper left arm. The bullet went straight through without damaging any vital nerves or veins, but he did have to have stitches in his head from being hit with the butt of the pistol. The hospital security called the police. The police arrived and Sean pressed charges against Lou. After a week, Sean called his grandmother to send for him and telling her that it was my fault he got shot. His Grandmother did send for him. "Lou received two years in prisons and probation for five years after serving his time."

Sean is back in Minneapolis for two weeks that gave him enough time to get involved with the same group of people that caused us problems before. This is now causing a lot more problems in our marriage. I arrived in Minneapolis a week after Sean had and we are living with his Grandparents until the apartment on the second floor is available. I'm attending college and active in the community. Sean thinks I'm wasting my time because I'm volunteering and not getting paid for the work I'm doing. He is not crazy about this at all and he is issuing alternatives: to stop or he will leave. I refuse to let him dictate my life, so I continued volunteering. I'm doing something positive and was not going to let his greed and insecurities interfere with what I'm doing. Sean packed and moved some place else. I did not want to take the apartment upstairs because he would try to us it to his advantage. Sean's Mother did not want me to move back to Texas so she insisted we move in with her and her husband. I hesitated for the same reason that I did not want to take the apartment upstairs above his Grandmother. Dee was able to convince me to move in. I knew she would not allow him to take advantage of the situation. We are more like Mother and daughter, so the arrangement would work out well. She said I could save my money and she would enjoy having my company. Sean thought this arrangement would keep me from dating but he is wrong. Dee did not mind me having male visitors. Sean had hidden the fact that he is living with an ex partner, but Dee thought I had the right to know. Dee pulled me aside and told me of Sean's living arrangement. She had always told me that I deserved better. With Sean living with someone else, I could not understand why he concerned himself with my life. He has been living with this person for the past three months and she is now pregnant with his child. After finding out Sean's secret, I am walking home from school and it started to rain. I took a route which took me about two blocks every day from where they lived. Just for the heck of it, I decided to go to their apartment. Walking up the stairs to the second floor, I walked into the apartment without knocking. I entered the living room and took a quick glance to see if Sean is in there. I did not see Sean but she is sitting on the sofa. I had been in this apartment before they move there, and I'm familiar with the interior. I walked passed her sitting on the sofa and went into the bedroom and never saying a word to her. Sean is asleep in the bed. I began waking him by shaking him and saying: "Get up, I need a ride home, it is raining outside." He jumped and sat up, rubbing his eyes to focus them. Once he had his eyes focused, he looked up at me and simply said: "OK" I at least expected him to ask me, what was I doing there? He got up and went into the bathroom to wash his face and started to get dressed while I was sitting on the end of the bed waiting. I was expecting her to enter the bedroom at anytime to see what is going on, but she never did. After he had finished dressing, we walked out into the living room, passing her again sitting in the same spot. Still she said nothing, nor did Sean say anything to her. I started to wonder what kind of relationship they have. We walked downstairs to a car, which turned out to be hers. I looked up to a window to see if she bothered even to look out to see us leaving in her car. I did not see her, so I don't know if she did or not. I still do not understand why she did not react. We drove off and I'm now waiting for Sean to say or ask me anything. He never said a word about what just happened. I only did this to show her how easy it would be for me to get him back. He drove me home, I did not expect him to even get out of the car, but he did. We went into the house and after a few hours I was waiting for him to leave to return back to her. Instead Sean got really comfortable, so comfortable that he did not leave. He stayed, for two weeks he stayed. He did not pick up the telephone once to call her. Finally he left and I knew when he disrespected both of us and that I did not want him back. She should wake up too. I never called or talked to him much after that, only to ask about getting a divorce. I realized it is finally over between Sean and me.

After three months my friends and I went to Cork's. It is Thursday night. The night the club featured male dancers, we would meet there almost every Thursday night to see Gorgeous George, Mystical Magical Michael and Chaz. My friends and I after the show ended we would go home but tonight I'm staying to met Ira. Ira and I met two months ago this Thursday and have been dating ever since. While I'm waiting, I could hear two individuals, standing in the balcony above me. They were discussing which one would come down to say something to me. I never looked up to see who they are and hoping they would not bother me at all. I listened to this conversation for about fifteen minutes and then they were quite. One appeared standing next to my seat. Still I never looking up at him, he says: "Hi, Why is a nice looking woman like you doing sit in this place all alone?" I answered: "I'm waiting for someone." He says: "Could I sit with you while you wait?" I answered: "No thank you but I rather you did not." Still I never looking up to see what he looked like and because I never looked up, all I could see was the bottom of his pants and his cow boy boots. He says: "I'm sorry for bothering you." Then he turned and walked away. Ira arrived after a few minutes. We danced and drank champagne, until eleven thirty p.m., then we drove to his condo. Ira and I spent every evening together and still have not consummated out relationship. I think he may not find himself interested in me that way. I'm not an unattractive woman, which makes it even harder to understand what the problem is. I'm hoping it is not due to some hidden prejudice, like race. Ira is a white male and I'm African American. When I asked him what, the problem is, he answered: "I do not want our relationship to be based on sex. When the time is right, I would like it to be special." This surprised me because usually the woman says this, not the man.

Two weeks has passed and Ira called me at work to tell me he would be picking me up earlier than usual today. Saying he has something planned for tonight. I went home and spent time with Sharon and Cherry. After putting the girls to bed and now they are sleeping, I took a long hot bath. An hour after my bath Ira arrived. Ira picked me up and we went straight to his condo to get dressed. Ira has purchased some clothing for me to wear out this evening; a light silk grays dress with snake skin trim on the neckline and the belt. Matching stockings, earrings, a slip and some perfume are there too. I dressed and Ira looked very pleased about how I looked in the clothes he purchased. Everything fit perfectly. Then Ira went to do the same. He enters the living room wearing a light gray sweater, gray slacks and a pair of gray snake skin shoes. Ira is a very handsome man to start but tonight he looks extremely handsome and he is all mine tonight. We are now on our way to Cork's. We drank champagne and danced until about eleven thirty p.m. Ira asked if I was ready to leave and I told him yes. We went back to his place. Not knowing Ira has chosen this to be that special night, we arrived and when I walked in I could not believe my eyes. Ira had catered in hors d'oeuvres, champagne and flowers. When entering the bedroom to change, I noticed on the bed there are rose pedal spread over the top of the sheets, with the comforter folded back. Lying at the foot of the bed is an off-white negligee with matching robe and slippers. I showered and put on the negligee and matching pieces. I walked into the living room and Ira begun smiling, saying: "You look lovely." He then went to do the same. He finished and entered the room wearing the sexiest red bikini drawers and a matching robe. We sat on the couch and began to enjoy soft music, food and champagne. He stood up, holding his hand out to take mine and gently pulled me from the couch. Pulling me close in his arms Ira began placing many passionate kisses on my lips, face and neck. Ira leads me into the bedroom where he began to make love to me, oh so gently. Ira was as gentle as if placing a rose pedal in the palm of your hand and not wanting to disturb or bruise it in anyway. My body exploded like fireworks on the forth of July. I thought to myself: "I'm glad I waited because the wait was worth it." He made me feel very special not just by making love to me but in every way. I'm very content with my relationship with Iran. We just fit.

Thinking it is time to talk with Sean, concerning a divorce. On Monday, I called Sean. Hoping Sean will not contest the divorce this time but of course he did. Sean did not want to discuss getting a divorce just like before. When I said divorce, he would get very angry and hung up the telephone. I called and Sean answered the telephone and the conversation was going OK until I mentioned divorce, then he hung up on me again. After that conversation he would avoid me at all cost.

A year has passed and Sean is still avoiding me. Even with him still living with someone else and now they have a new baby. He still is not ready to let me go, so I continued with my relationship with Ira and pretending I'm free.

It is Friday night. I dressed and now ready to go to Cork's nightclub. Ira will join me there later. I finished dressing and the telephone starts to ring. Putting the receiver to my ear, I could hear my youngest sister's voice, but could not understand what she is saying very well. Rae seems apparently upset about something. Her father, Mr. James, has become very ill over the pass year. Suffering from cancer that had taken over his whole body and now he has taken a turn for the worst. Rae was calling me to let me know that the doctor did not expect Mr. James to make it through the night. I told her that I will take the next available flight out. Mr. James and I over the pass few years had gotten very close. He became a second Dad. I hung up the telephone and called Ira to let him know what was happening and after speaking with Ira, he purchased airline tickets for me to leave. When I arrived, Rae is waiting at the airport. I approached her and could see the tears on her face. Rae then told me that Mr. James did not make it through the night that he passed away at eleven forty-five tonight. The news hit me very hard. I than held onto Rae because I felt the loss as much as she did. When I reached Mom's house, I called Ira to tell him of the bad news. He had not met Mom, Dad or Mr. James. Ira spoke with Mom several times before I left Minneapolis and after I arrive in Amarillo. I will be here at least two weeks just to make sure Mom and Rae was OK.

When I arrived back to Minneapolis, Ira was here at the gate waiting for me. "How are you doing? And your Mom,

How is she doing? I told him I'm OK, but I'm worried about Mom. He says: 'If you need to return, just let me know.' I said 'OK' Ira then replied: 'I would like to take you and the girls out to dinner if you are up to it.' I answered: "That would be great, the girls will love it."

Ira picked us up at six thirty and we had supper at Ciatti's. Ira and I took Sharon and Cherry to the arcade to play video games. They are having a great time. It is now ten o'clock and then took them home. Sharon and Cherry went to bed. Ira and I watched television and talked most of the night. We fell asleep on the living room floor but when the back door opened it woke us the next morning. Sean appeared, looking down and standing over us. He had a really strange look in his eyes. Sean gave the look that I'm familiarly with, especially when he is angry. He is very angry and trying not to show it. Ira noticed the look Sean is giving me and asks: "Will you be all right when I leave, if you do not feel comfortable, I will stay for a while?" 'I told him to go on that I will be fine.' Knowing as long as Dee is home, Sean would not try anything. Ira left but he called from his car phone to check on me. Sean never said anything. He just starred at me strangely. The stares at one time did frighten me but now they just let me know I have made him mad. Sean left ten minutes later, never saying a word to me.

It is the Winter of 1980, on a Thursday. I'm not feeling very well. My best friend, Lucy called and wants to go to Cork's. The way I'm feeling, I know I should not go any where but she was able to talk me into going. Before Lucy called, Ira had called to see how I'm feeling. I told him that I'm not feeling very well and planned to stay home. Ira is telling me I need to take care of my cold before it got any worst. Lucy picked me up thirty minutes later. We arrived at Cork's and I'm still feeling really bad. I have been here a few minutes and standing near the DJ booth when I spotted Ira heading toward me. When he got close enough, he said: "I knew you would be here. Why didn't you say home and take care of that cold?" With me knowing he was right, but with me being stubborn and cranky, I said: 'Just turn around, walk away and do not say a damn thing to me.' He keeps trying to talk to me but I'm in no mood for a lecture. Getting angrier, I'm screaming at him; 'Just turn around, walk away and do not say a damn thing to me.' I walked away from him and headed out of the door to walk home with him following behind me. As I'm walking home, Ira is following me in his car and trying to convince me to get into the car because it is so cold. With me refusing, he follows me until I'm safely home. Finally I made it home, cold but safe. Looking behind me, I could see Ira turning his car around to leave. Not wanting to admit it I was glad he followed me home. Once inside I went upstairs to start my bath and check on my daughter. After getting settled in the warm tub and feeling very relaxed, I asked my self; 'Why was I so mean to Ira?' He is only being concerned. I will call him when I finished with my bath and apologize for my behavior toward him. Picking up the receiver to call, but there is no answer. I will try calling him again later. I tried again and still there is no answer. I will wait until morning to try again.

It is now seven A.M., I called Ira and still there is no answer this morning. I will call his office. Ira's secretary answers the telephone, saying: 'Ira has not arrived as of yet and she will make sure that he gets my message.' I dressed and left for work, I waited until about ten o'clock for Ira to return my call but he did not call back yet. I picked up the telephone to call him again. His secretary again answers the telephone. She says: 'Ira called in for his messages because he will not be in today and that he will be flying out of town for a meeting by one thirty p.m. today.' 'He did get your message and said he will call you when he finished with his meeting.' Hanging up the telephone wondering if Ira is angry with me for the way I acted last night. He has every right to be angry.

I waited for Ira to call me all afternoon but never heard from him. I waited for days and still never heard one word from him. His secretary called every other day, saying: "Ira is still in meetings and he will call you soon." I replied: "I have waited long enough for him to call me and you can tell him not to worry about calling me any more." She tried hard to plead his case, wanting me to wait to hear from him. I have tried to be patient but I will wait no longer.

My employer is giving a social function at the Riverview Supper Club today after work. The employees could bring a family member or friend along if he or she chooses. My supervisor brought her brother. I had no ideal that her brother is the same person who tried to talk with me months ago at Cork's. After holding a conversation with him is when I realized it was indeed he. Edward Sutton is his name. Edward and I talked and danced a few times but before we parted, he asked if he could come take me to lunch sometimes. I told him it would be fine. We went out a few times for lunch before we started to date seriously. We would take the children's places and spent lots of time with his family.

Just when Edward and I have gotten to be more than friends, I finally received a call from Ira. Ira started to explain why I had not heard from him, saying; 'The night, I followed you home from Cork's well I went back there.' Right when Cork's is closing, an ex-girl friend asked me for a ride home. When I pulled up into the drive way to let her out, some guy came out. The person robbed me and stabbed me several times. One of the stabs hit me half an inch from my heart. I remained conscious long enough to drive myself to the hospital. I collapsed in the parking lot of the hospital and was unconscious until a week ago, but I'm still in the Intensive Care Unit. I was not able to call you until I was strong enough to talk. My secretary did not know I'm in the hospital until I was able to call her. 'She could not tell you where I was because she did not know herself, so she took it upon herself to tell you something.' I replied: "So you are telling me you have been unconscious until a few days ago? I'm sorry you were put through this." With concern I asked: "How are you doing now and will you have any permanent disabilities from this?" He answered: "The doctor says I will recover without any permanent disabilities but I will have to take it easy for a while to let my body heal. I'm sorry you were kept in the dark." I could not say a word, now that I know the truth. He then asked: "Are we still going to be together or have you moved on with your life?" I answered: "I think it is best we did not, especially with all you have gone through and you need to focus on getting better. It will take all your energy to heal. 'I would like to be able to call to check on you from time to time.' "If it is OK with you."

Edward and I have gotten very close. I have not called Ira in more than two weeks because my focus is on Edward now.

Six months has passed. Edward and I have gotten serious. We have discussed moving in together. We both have children and this decision will change their lives too. We made the decision with their blessings. Steven and Natalie are Edward's Children. To top it all off, we are both married to other people and separated from them for years. We planned to divorce them immediately.

We decided to make the move. Everything is working out with us living together. The people who know us were sure we had married already because we live as though we are. We just do not have the legal document saying so.

The burglar's targeted our home many times during a year's time. The house is vacant for at least a year before we moved into it. Now I know why. The house has many hidden problems and the landlord neglected telling us about them before or after we rented it. I sent letters to the landlord many times asking him to repair the problems but we never received any response from him of any kind. After many attempts to reach the landlord or getting the repairs done, I asked Edward to speak with him. I worried about the safety of my family and fear that the house could catch on fire from the bad wiring. I felt I had no other choice but to make a report to the Department of Housing Inspectors. The Inspector returned my call and made an appointment with me to inspect the house. After a full inspection of the house's interior, the inspector found many problems other then the ones I had complained about. Under the Standard Housing Living Codes the house is unlivable. Two weeks after the inspection the landlord received a copy of the report before I had the chance to show Edward my copy the landlord informed Edward about me reporting him to the Housing Inspectors. The notice gave him thirty days to make all the necessary repairs before the deadline or they will condemn the house. Edward returned home from meeting with the landlord and he is very angry with me for making the report. This added to the anger he had for not being able to save money, now angrier because we have to look for another house within thirty days. He is threatening to move back in with his Mom. Now receiving a letter from the landlord and him is claiming he is not financially able to make the repairs angered Edward. With Edward being angry he again threatened to move in with his Mom. Two weeks passed before we heard from the inspector. The letter finally came by mail containing the condemned notice, affected immediately. Between receiving this notice telling us, we will need to look for another home and with more burglaries in our home angered Edward even more. Edward is so angry that again he says for the third times: "I'm moving home to my Mother. I have had enough." Edward's voice convinced me by the way it sounded that he meant it this time that he will be moving to his Mom's house. Believing that he did mean it I made plans to move to my Mom's because I could not maintain this large house finance with my income.

It is morning and I'm doing my every weekday routine getting the children ready for nursery and public school. The difference this morning is I will not be sending Sharon and Cherry to school. I got Steven and Natalie dressed, while Edward dressed to attend his classes, too. Sharon and Cherry dressed themselves. After Edward left with Steven and Natalie, I drove to the bank to withdraw the money I have saved. The money I saved for surprising Edward with to get a new or newer car. He is always underneath the two cars we have been working on them. A newer car would eliminate this headache. Instead I will have to use the money to go to Texas. Heading back home to pack so Sharon, Cherry and I could take the next flight to Texas.

In two days I have gotten a job and an apartment. Edward called me regularly. I guess he misses me as much as I miss him, and after being in Amarillo for two weeks, Edward, Steven and Natalie came to join us. I have a job position as the Apartment Manager, where I now live. Edward got a job working as a full time Army Reservist. Everything is going really well for us. After a year had passed, we received a call from Edward's sister, Nettie and she began telling Edward that their Mother has suffered a stroke. Edward became devastated and after finishing up the call from his sister, we began packing to return to Minneapolis, immediately. We arrived there and headed directly to the hospital to see his Mom. After she was able to see Edward, she made a speedy recovery and released from the hospital less than a week later. She had no noticeable signs from the stroke. We stayed with his Mother until she regained her strength.

After six months, I'm ready to be in my own place. After going to several apartment complexes, I'm able to choice one I really liked. We moved and Edward has started a new job. After about four months Edward is very quiet and I wonder if he is having problems at work because I cannot think of anything else that could be bothering him. We are not having problems between us, either. I really do not know why his is not talking to me.

It is the fourth of July and we have invited our family members over for a barbecue to celebrate. I arranged the furniture in order for us to sit together instead of two separate rooms. Everyone is here and seems to be enjoying themselves. Edward seems to be having a good time, at least when he was talking with the others but when I talked with him, he became quiet again. I do not think I have done anything to make him act this way toward me. Something definitely is bothering him. I will let him be for now. It is late and everyone has begun to leave. Our family members slowly moving because of all the food they ate and tired from playing games. The barbecue was a success and now I can start the clean up. I have gotten the children into bed and I can take a long hot bath. After my bath and in my pajamas, I entered the living room to ask Edward if he is ready to go to bed. His reply caught me off guard, saying: "I'm sleeping on the couch until the furniture is returned back to their original places." I could not believe what he just said to me. I know he did not get this attitude because I changed the furniture around. Now I'm angry and say to him: "If you are sleeping on the couch then I will go get someone to sleep with me in the bed." Knowing this would make him angry. Edward stood up, never saying another word. He walked into the children's room taking Natalie and Steven from their beds, putting them into the van. Edward began to load the rest of their things into the van as well. Still not uttering a word and with the babies crying, he drove off. I'm angry as well as puzzled and still not knowing what happened to make him act this way.

Waking up the next morning and still do not have a clue as to what happened last night. I'm missing them terribly and wanted to call to talk to Edward, but I wanted him to suffer as I'm. I got dressed and then heard a knock at the door. Dee has sent Sean, of all people to bring me to her. Dee's Mother has taken ill and is asking to see me.

Ten o'clock and I'm returning home. When we drove up, I could see Edward is here waiting and he wants to talk. After talking with him for an hour, I realized that we will not be getting back together. Then I told him that I will be moving back to Texas and I will be leaving this weekend.

Edward did not seem to be happy about me leaving but chose not to try to stop me from doing it.

It is Friday, August 1984. I packed my things and now waiting for Edward. Edward arrived an hour before my bus is to leave. As we loaded the luggage in the van, we were unusually quiet probably waiting for the other to speak first. We arrived in enough time to say our good byes. Edward moves in close to me to give me a kiss good bye. He then leans over to give Sharon and Cherry a hug and kiss. We boarded the bus and it is backing out from the parking lot with the girls and me looking out at him standing there and waving bye. My eyes filled with tears as did Sharon and Cherry. They continued to wave, cry and saying: "Bye, Daddy." They then turned to me saying: "Mom, do we have to go. We don't want to leave Daddy." Thinking to myself, it is best seeing how they are reacting to leaving him. They would have a harder time if we stayed.

Sharon, Cherry and I arriving in Amarillo on Monday and them are continuing to ask: 'Why did we have to leave them behind?' I'm not answering, not knowing how to answer them as of yet. My sister, Rae met us at the bus station. She to could not understand why Edward and I have broken up after all these years.

Right away I applied for a job and hired on the spot at C. R. Anthony's department store. I have gotten an apartment in the same complex as my Mother. Within a week I had my apartment completely furnished.

Three months in my apartment and everything is moving right alone but I'm missing Edward, Natalie and Steven very much. I have not heard from him since I arrived in Texas, so I assumed he has gone on with his life and forgotten about us. By this time, Mike has found out I'm back in the city. He visited many times. We are now involved again. Mike was the first person I ever dated. I cared for him a lot and getting involved with him will help heal the wounded heart from the break up with Edward. Trying not to think about Edward was hard work. Mike and I started after four months have been discussing marriage. Everyone who went to school with us believed we should have married long ago. Mike has a problem with jealousy and he is now starting to have problems with it again. I heard that if you cannot trust the one you love then whys stay with them at all. The jealousy made it hard to continue the relationship and it quickly came to an end. I could not handle it any longer.

I still have Edward in my heart, but still trying to live my life. My sister; Cindy and Jade wanted to take me out tonight to a club where all my old friends hung out at. I stood around for about fifteen minutes when a young man approached me. He says his name is Rocky Tinson. I talked with him long enough to realize he is the brother of my sister-in-law, Debbie. Rocky asked me to dance. We danced and talked most of the night and before we parted he asked for my telephone number. Rocky would call every day to talk and sometimes to ask if he could take me to the movies, dinner or dancing. This went on for months, even with continuing interference from his ex-girl friend. They have a son that she used every chance she has. She is trying her best to keep him away from me. I have tried not to say anything about the games she is playing, but enough is enough and I have reached my limit. Rocky is either afraid to say anything fears she may not let him sees his son or he did not believe me.

Sharon is starting to have problems with her asthma again. I have always trusted the doctors in Minneapolis that gave me a reason to move back to Minnesota. I also wanted to be near Edward and the children again. Rocky has enough problems and I did not want to take him along because I am hoping Edward has not married and maybe he and I could get back together. It has been eight months since I have spoken to Edward.

Rocky manages to talk me into allowing him to come along. We arrived in Minneapolis in February of 1985. I had made arrangement before hand to take over the duplex that a friend of mine is moving out of. She moved out the same day we arrived. Rocky is working within a week after arriving back in Minneapolis and I'm attending class at Twin Cities Opportunity Industrialization Center. I decided that it is best that Edward not knows I'm back in the city with Rocky being here with me. Seeing or hearing Edward's voice would make it hard to stay away from him. More than I wanted to admit it anyone else is only a substitute for him.

Rocky and I are watching televisions one night and the children are sleeping. We heard a knock at the door downstairs. I thought to myself: 'Who on earth could this be knocking on my door at two A.M.?' I asked: "Who is it? It is very hard to hear what the person is saying because the voice is coming from down stairs. As I'm heading down the stairs, I asked again: 'Who is it?' I still could not hear the voice clear enough too recognize who it is. I continued walking down the stair until I'm close enough to the door to hear better than I asked again: 'Who is it?' Now hearing the person very clear, I could not believe who it is. It is Edward. I thought to myself: 'What on Earth is he doing?' 'How did he find out that I'm back in town?' Pulling myself together before I opened the door. I opened the door and there he stood and I said to him; 'Hi, come on in.' This is all I could get out of my mouth because I became speechless. I turned around and headed up the stairs with him following me. I could not believe he is here and whoever told him that I returned neglected to tell him that I brought someone with me. I did not know what to do once I got him inside. As we entered the living room, I began to introduce Edward to Rocky. It startled Edward, because he did not expect to find someone else in my house, so he quickly apologized for coming by so late, saying; 'I just wanted to see my girls.' I then turned and headed down the hall way to show him the location of the girl's bedroom. Edward entered their room and gently kissed them both on the cheek and saying to them in a whispering voice, 'Daddy, loves both of you girls very much.' He then returned to the living room, where Rocky and I are still watching television. Edward apologized again as he starts toward the door to leave. I followed him down the stairs to lock the door after him. When we reached the door Edward turned around and looked into my eyes, saying: 'I still love you, Ellen.' He then turned and went out the door to his car, leaving me standing here with my heart in my hand and mouth wide open. I went back up the stairs to the living room. Rocky did not say anything. He just looked at me. What he saw is all he needed to see. Our relationship went down hills after that. Two months later Rocky returned to Amarillo, after receiving a call from his son's Mother. She used the baby's hospitalization to get Rocky to come back to Amarillo. Rocky arrived in Amarillo and found out the hospitalization was a lie and his son is as healthy as a horse. Rocky called to let me know that he would be returning in a week, I insisted he stays in Amarillo. I sent the rest of his other belongs to him later. He needs to be there for his son anyway and I wanted to see Edward again.

Edward and I have been seeing each other again for two months with no commitment until he called me one day saying: "I'm going to start seeing someone else." It hurt me so bad but I appreciated his honesty. What made it so bad is that earlier today, I found out that I'm pregnant with his child. I thought it is best he not know because he wants to see someone else. I wanted him to be with me because he loves me not because I'm carrying his child. Not one day went by that I did not consider calling Edward to tell him. I just did not want him to think I wanted to trap him into a relationship he did not want.

CHAPTER THREE

Door number two closing with,
Door number three is slowly opening.

I'm quite busy with Sharon, her asthma had become worst and she spent a lot of time in the hospital. The doctors told me that Sharon would never be able to have children. Her lungs and heart muscles sustained a lot of damaged because of the stress to try to breathe. After a month or two, Sharon had seemed to be getting a little better, not having as many visits to the hospital. I had a chance to get out and take a break from everything. Debra, my neighbor and I went to Moby Dick's club. It was my first time there. Right as we entered the door way of the club, a young man approached me. He very boldly leaned in close to my ear. He whispered: 'I really would like to get to know you.' I looked over his shoulder and standing behind him is a very attractive man. I pushed him aside, saying: "I want to get to know him." I pointed in the direction of the person standing behind him. The young man who had whispered in my ear said: "This is my cousin, Juan." He looks disappointed and proceeded to introduce Juan to me. Juan and I sat at the table and talked most of the night. I think he became interested in me by the way he talked. I let him know what I'm going through and I also told him that I'm two months' pregnant. This did not seem to bother him at all and before I left the club Juan asks if he could give me a call sometimes. I told him it would be OK and wrote down my telephone number to give to him. With all of the changes I am going through it would be nice to have someone to talk to.

Two days after I had met Juan, he gave me a call and asked if he could come over to see me this weekend and maybe go see a movie. I told him it would be fine and he will have the opportunity to meet my two daughters.

It is now nine thirty A.M. Saturday morning, when the telephone rang. I picked the telephone up and heard Juan's voice on the other end, saying: 'Good morning.' 'May I speak to Ellen please?' Realizing who it is, I answered: "This is she speaking. Hello, Juan. How are you doing?" He replied: "I'm doing better now that I have heard your voice. I'm calling to see what would be a good time to come over and also to get directions to your place." Two o'clock will be fine. This will give me enough time to get my girls taken care of: I answered. Juan arrived at two o'clock on the dot, ringing my buzzer downstairs. After he entered the apartment, I asked if I could get him something to drink. I called the girls to come into the living room so that I can introduce them to him.

The four of us talked for about two hours then Juan suggested that we go to see a movie and out for a bit to eat. The day went very well and after we arrived back to the apartment I helped Sharon and Cherry gets ready for bed. Juan and I talk for about an hour more until he said it is getting late and I should leave. Sharon and Cherry said good night and went off to bed and I walked him downstairs to the door. We said good bye and I thanked him for a very nice day. He asked: "Can I call you tomorrow and if it is OK, I would like to come over again? I told him to call and I will check to see if I had something planned already or not. He turned to head toward his car and turned around for the last time to say and wave good bye. I went back to my apartment to retire for the night.

It is now July of 1985, Juan and I have been dating for five weeks and he has already asked me to marry him. I said, yes! , I will marry you. We started to make plans for our wedding in August. I had gotten my divorce from Sean while Edward and I were living in Amarillo. Sharon is still having problems but not as bad but Cherry is now having asthma symptoms. I took Cherry to the doctor and he did confirm that she is asthmatic. I worried with both of my daughters now suffer with this illness. I hope Cherry's asthma is not as severe as Sharon's.

Juan and I decided to marry on August 1. I now have two weeks to make all the arrangement.

August 1, Juan and I married as planned. There were some very strange things that happen today before the ceremony. (1) Sean took us to pick up our wedding cake and while driving us Sean is trying to convince Juan not to marry me. Obviously, it did not work. 2) Sean's family attended the ceremony, his mother, sister and brother. After the wedding everyone gathered at our apartment for the reception.

Six months now and Juan and I still act like newly weds. Sharon and Cherry asked if they could go to the Kid's Community Center located behind our apartment building. Sharon asthma limited her physical activities. Her involvement at the center never crossed my mind. I talked with one of the social workers from the club and she convinces me she would not let Sharon participate in any physical activities. I agreed to let Sharon go. Cherry has to finish her homework before she is able to go. It is now eight p.m. Sharon returned home. She sat down to eat her favorite food spaghetti and meatballs when finish she headed to her room to prepare for her bath. I heard Sharon calling for me and when I reached her I could see that she is having problems with her asthma. She has a different look in her eyes that I had never seen before and it frightened me. I ran to my bedroom to call for an ambulance and dressed as I spoke with the 9-1-1 operator. Just as I'm finishing with the 9-1-1 call, Sharon called for me again. I rushed back to her side and Juan is bringing her down the hall way to the living room. The hall way is too narrow for the stretcher to come through. With the telephone still in my hand I dialed my sister's telephone number and when she answered I told her what is happening. When I finished speaking with Carolyn, I went to Sharon. Sharon eyes filled with tears. She then spoke with a calmed voice. She says: "Mom, I'm dying." She then collapsed in Juan's arms. I'm frantic and running back and forth to watch for the ambulance. It seems like hours when it has only been seconds before the ambulance arrived. The paramedics immediately began working on Sharon because her lung has collapsed and there is no heartbeat. By the time Carolyn and Barb arrived the paramedics had not been able to get Sharon to respond. They continued until Sharon stabilized enough to transport to the hospital. Even at the hospital the doctors worked hard to sustain her, but are not able to revive her. After two hours the doctor appeared and when I looked at his face I knew my baby died. I manage to pull myself together because I

have to be able to tell Cherry about her sister. I asked Barb
to bring Cherry home because I wanted to be the one to tell
her. When Cherry arrived home, she looked in my face and
she knew her sister did not survive. She grabbed me and we
held each other tightly afraid to let go for fear of losing each
other. Now it is time for me to call my family in Texas and
call Anthony too. I did not have Anthony's telephone number because he made it a point for me not to have it.
Anthony did not want me to have contact with my son. He
has kept him from me for the past seven years. I'm not
looking forward to having a conversation with him, but he
has a right to know what has happened. I will call his parents since I do have their telephone number. I hope it has
not changed. His Mother answered the telephone and I
began telling her about Sharon passing and she showed no
remorse. She told me she did not have Anthony's telephone
number and that I need to call his sister, Faith. I called Faith
and she is being very nasty on the telephone until I'm able
to get a word in. After explaining to her the reason for me
calling, Faith then gives me Anthony's home telephone
number. I called and Anthony answers the telephone. I
quickly told him Sharon had died and how. His replied:
"What do you want me to do about it?" It shocked me so
bad I could not say a word and just hung up the telephone.
I swore never to talk to him again. Anthony called right
back but Juan had to talk with him and together they made
all the arrangement for Sharon's services. I'm in no shape to
handle this.

Sharon's' friends and other associates came to our house
to offer their sympathy to Cherry and me the following day.
My parent arrived the next day along with two of my sisters.
Edward's Mother came by today and right away she noticed

that I'm pregnant. Edward's Mother placed her hand on my stomach and asked: "Does Edward know that you are pregnant?" I answered: "No." She reached for the telephone and proceeded to call Edward to tell him about me being pregnant. She never asked if the baby is Edward. Within an hour Edward showed up at my door and wanted to talk but I told him we will discuss this at a later date. I could tell that he is having a hard time with Sharon passing. Edward is the person whom Sharon knew as her Dad because he was with her from the time she was six years old.

Anthony arrived with DJ, his wife and their son two days later. He and I did not talk at first until he wanted to know about Sharon. He had not seen the girls since they were one and three years of age. Cherry ran away from him when he would approach her for a day or so. I told her who he is and she eventually felt comfortable enough to talk to him. DJ is hesitant with me for a while but soon felt comfortable with me and did not want to leave my side. I could see that the relationship between him and his Father is not too good and he has a lot of anger in him. Cherry showed some resentment toward Anthony too for keeping her brother from us. I resented him for cheating me to see DJ grows to be this handsome young individual. From the time DJ was born he looked a lot like his Father but now he could pass for my twin, looking more like me than I do. I could not understand why Anthony wanted to keep him because it had to be a constant reminder of me every day he looked at DJ.

Anthony and I went into the bedroom that Cherry and Sharon shared. He asked me many questions about Sharon and what she was like. This will never take the place of actually knowing her because she was special in so many ways. The guilt he is feeling he has to live with it for the rest of his life.

Two weeks after Sharon had passed and everyone's returned back to their homes now it is time for me to try and get Cherry and my life back to some kind of normalcy.

I had not felt my baby moving much inside of my stomach and I made an appointment to see the doctor. After the exam the doctor told me to go to the hospital for an ultra sound. When he checked the ultra sound and I saw the look on his face, I knew something is wrong. He then told me that my baby is stillborn. I managed though the tears to ask what caused it. He answered: "The toxemia caused swelling and fluid to build up which cut off the oxygen for the baby. The stress from losing Sharon did not help the situation. I'm admitted into the hospital and then taken to surgery the same day. The baby is a girl and now I have lost two daughters. As soon as I'm able, I called Edward first. Edward arrived at the hospital a half and hour later. The doctor explained to him what had happened. Edward is so upset. After he left, I called Juan. I did not want Juan and Edward together here. I had complications with my blood pressure and did not want it to get any worst. I will be released from the hospital hopefully in two days. My body continued with the pregnancy cycles which made it hard to hold myself together at times. 'More than anything, I wanted Edward here with me.'

Still having a hard time with the reality, Sharon is no longer with us. I caught myself still setting a place for her at the dinner table. I even called for her and Cherry to come take baths. Cherry will not go into her bedroom anymore. She will not even go stay over night with her cousin either because she is too afraid to leave my side as I'm to leave her side. Juan is being pushed away ignored almost. He is trying too hard to help us through the grief. He is trying so hard that it made me angry. Cherry, Juan and I tried counseling but it made me even angrily than I'm already. I refused to continue the counseling after the second session. I have become abusive with Juan with words and sometime physically. I have no right and before it gets out of hand I asked Juan to leave. Juan does not agree with the decision I made but I left him no choice. After Juan moved out he began stalking me. He broke into the apartment and made threatening phone calls. I called the police and went to obtain an Order for Protection against him. Juan ignored the order's time and time again. I called the police but the officer explained that if he has left the premises they could not arrest him. I think Juan knows this because he would leave before the police arrived.

A week later while moving my nineteen-inch television my legs collapsed under me while at the same time I experienced pain in my lower back. I called for an ambulance to take me to the hospital and after finding out that I will be hospitalized. I called Juan to watch Cherry. I remained in the hospital for nine days. The doctor completed the tests and said that he could not determine the cause of the problem. The doctor released me from the hospital the next day. I'm getting ready to go to the laundry mat and I went to check my hiding place where I kept my money. The money is mostly for Christmas Shopping, but I needed to use some for the laundry. I checked the hiding place for the money and there is no money. Apparently Juan had gone through my things and found the money and had taken it. When I confronted him, he agreed to replace it. He replaced half of it then I told him to stay away from us. I went to the laundry mat and Juan showed up there asking me if he could come back home. I told him, no. He than put his hand into his coat pocket and pulled out a gun. He pointed the gun at me and at the same time, saying: "If I cannot have you, no one else will." I'm too angry to be frightened and says to him: "If you shoot me, you better make sure you kill me because if you don't, I will come back for you." The owner of the laundry saw the gun and called the police. The police arrived quickly surrounding him. Two of the officers searched him and did not find the gun right away until I told them to check the lining of his coat. The officer located the gun and placed Juan under arrest. One of the officers stayed behind to take down statements from everyone that is here. Two hours passed and I'm back home. The telephone rang and I answered it to Juan's voice. He says: "I'm out." I hung up the telephone, quickly. I could not believe that he called. The police must have released him without taking him before the judge. I then decided that the only way I will be able to get away from him is to move and change my name. I filed for my divorce and did just that.

CHAPTER FOUR

Having to slam door number three,
I'm a little afraid of opening door number four.

I have decided after all I have gone through, to take some time out to get my children and myself together.

A year and a half have passed and I have accomplished what I wanted for Cherry, DJ and myself. Anthony called asking Cherry to come spend the summer with him and I want DJ to come to spend the summer with me.

It is Friday, March 5. Pam, Marci and I decided to go out and celebrate Pam's birthday today. We met at Marci's house and from there we headed to Moby Dick's Lounge. We are in the back because located there is the dance floor. We stood near the bar for an hour when a young man approached me and introduced himself, saying: 'Hello, My name is Lloyd Simm.' 'Would you like to dance?' Holding his hand out for me to take and he leads me to the dance floor. We did not talk much until we were off the dance floor and headed back to where Marci and Pam are standing. He began talking, asking me: "What is your name?" I answered: "My name is Kay." This has to be your first time in this place because I have never seen you before, he says. I answered: "Yes, it is my first time. My girl friends and I are celebrating because the today is Pam's birthday." He then excused himself and disappeared into the crowd of people. Pam and Marci excited about how good looking he is and asks me: 'Are you interested in him?' I told them no because I really had not thought about. He left disappearing into the crowd. He returned after a few songs played carrying drinks for all of us. I dance with him until half an hour before the club is to close. Lloyd then escorted us out and walked to the curb to flag down a taxi. Before I got into the taxi, he asked: "Could I call you sometime?" I answered: "Yes" and writing down my home telephone number to give to him. This is the second time that I have given my telephone number out the first time meeting them. I usually give out the number to the Police Station but never my home. I arrived home and as I walked into the apartment, and I could hear my telephone ringing. I ran upstairs to answer it so that I could get undressed while talking. It is Lloyd and he has made it home and called me right away. I said: "Hello." He then says: "I could not wait until later today to call you. I wanted to say good night." I replied: "That is thoughtful but I have to let you go now because I have to get rested for school tomorrow. You may call me after I get home." He said: "OK, good night and pleasant dreams."

After a long day at school I arrived home about six that evening and I could hear the telephone ringing as I unlocked the door. I picked up the telephone and could tell that it is Lloyd's voice over the phone. He says: "Hello, may I speak to Kay." I answered: "This is her speaking." He asks: "How was your day at school?" I answered: "Busy, I just walked into the house and heard the phone was ringing."

He says: "I'm sorry. I waited until now to call so you would have a few minutes before I called. I guess my timing was off." I replied: "It is OK." Then he asked: "Would it be all right if I came over to visit you later? I will not stay long because I know that you have to go to school tomorrow." I answered: "I do not think that is a good ideal." He asks: "Please, I will not stay long. I would like to talk with you for at least an hour or two." I said: "OK, just for an hour or two." I hung up the telephone and put on some comfortable clothes to cook dinner in. Cherry and I ate dinner. After she had finished with her dinner, she headed upstairs to take a bath while I cleaned the kitchen. At seven thirty p.m., Lloyd is knocking at the door. Lloyd entered, I took his coat to hang up and offered him some refreshments. Cherry came downstairs to see who is knocking and I introduced her to Lloyd. The three of us talked until Cherry says: "Mom, it is time for me to go to bed." As she headed to the staircase she stopped and turned to Lloyd and says: "Good night, Lloyd and I'm glad I met you." He said: "Good night, Cherry and I hope I get to see you again." Cherry started up the stairs to go to bed. Lloyd then looked at me and said: "I really hope I do get to see Cherry and you again." I did not know at that point if it is possible or not because we had talked about our age differences. The problem is that I'm at least seven years older than he is and I have a really hard time with dating younger man especially since I had married Sean. Lloyd did not have a problem with our age difference, saying: "Age is nothing but a number and you should not let that keep up from seeing each other." I told him that sometimes numbers can get you into trouble. Lloyd laughed but is very serious. At least he did not lie about his age as did Sean. I told Lloyd that I will have to think about this before I jump into another relationship. He says: "Don't let our ages make us miss out on something that could be good." After that statement I told him it is getting late and he should leave now, but I nearly had to drag him out of my apartment. He has finally left. I thought about what he said over and over again. Then finally realize that I'm hesitant because deep down in my heart there are feelings for Edward still. Edward is still a part of my life, not the way I would like him to be but we spoke regularly.

I called my Mom today to ask what she thought about dating a younger man and to tell her about Lloyd. Mom says: 'I would not date a younger person but you are a young woman.' Some young individuals do have their heads on straight and are able to love you like you deserve to be loved. In this case falling in love within reasonable limits of age differences should not make a difference. I always listen to Mom's advice because she has been through enough to have the wisdom. When I hung up the telephone with Mom, I found myself thinking about maybe consider-ing dating Lloyd. I considered it even if dating Lloyd is against my better judgment. I also came to the conclusion that all I will ever be is just a close friend to Edward.

The next day, Lloyd called to see if he could come over to visit again but today I'm not feeling very well. I'm in bed with the flu. It hit me all at once. Cherry talked with him and telling him I'm really sick. I woke up to Lloyd standing by my bed. He asked: "How are you feeling? I just looked up at him wondering; what is he doing? Then Cherry spoke up, saying: 'Mom, you were really sick and I was scared.' When Lloyd called, I told him you were sick and he came right away. 'He also brought you some cough syrup, juice and soup.' I looked over at Lloyd and thanked him for what he has done. He said: 'I'm glad I could help out.' Lloyd became a regular habit that I needed after that day. Soon as he is off work he would come here.

It is April 1. Cherry and I had agreed to ask Lloyd to move in, since he is here every day anyway. Cherry and I are very fond of him. A week later Lloyd moves in. I called Edward to let him know that Lloyd is here now and he called less. Soon Edward did not call at all unless it is concerning Natalie and Steven.

I heard from Edward after two months. Edward called to let me know that he is getting married in August. Again Edward has put a knife in my heart. No one will ever love him as I do and he will find that out. With him deciding to get married, it is time to let him go on with his life and I do the same as well. I'm angry and resentful that he would even consider marrying someone else with all we have gone through with over the years. I could not get up enough nerves to congratulate him because I would not have meant it. I will have a hard time letting him go.

It is now June 1988. Lloyd and I are getting alone just fine. Cherry and I are really close to him now. Cherry is packing to go visit with her father while DJ is coming here to visit with me for the summer. Cherry arrived in Texas on Friday and DJ arrived here on Saturday. Lloyd spent a lot of time with DJ as well as I did. I could still see DJ is holding on to a lot of anger. I did not want to force him to talk about it. I will wait until he is ready. He would lay his head on my lap or my shoulder and I could tell that any day now he will be ready to talk. I understood that I may not want to hear what he has to say but I will answer any question he may want to ask.

After being here for two weeks, DJ is ready to express his feeling and thoughts. He asks: "Mom, why did you just take my sisters and not me too?" I became shock that Anthony would put this thought in DJ's head. I took a deep breath before answering him. I finally answered him: "I did not leave you behind, your father came and took you away when you were five years old." DJ is now twelve years old. He replied: "Dad, told me you did not want me, just the girls." Anthony telling DJ all this lies angered me and I decided than to tell DJ how things happened the way they did and in other words the whole true. DJ looked at me with disbelief at first but after he is able to recall different events from his memory it changed his mind. The anger he was holding toward me has now turned to his Father. I had no plans to go into the details about his Dad and my marriage because it would hurt them to know what happened and make them look at their Father through angry eyes. I had no choice now but to tell DJ the truth. I did not want my child to hate me because of the lies Anthony had feed to him over the past seven years. I called Anthony to tell him about the conversation between DJ and me. I confronted him about the lies he told. Anthony would not talk with me after he could tell by my voice volume raised and hung up the phone. I had talked with Cherry several times since she has been with her father and she seems to be having a good time until Anthony began telling her lies about me. Lies that Cherry knew were lies.

The summer is ending. Anthony has sent for DJ to return home. Cherry is already back home. DJ asked if he could stay but Anthony told him no. I called DJ several times and Anthony would not let me speak to him. The last time I tried to call DJ the telephone number changed or disconnected. I did not have any other way to reach DJ. Anthony has taken him away from me again.

It is August. Edward called to talk to me and I did not know why. Edward is still getting married as far as I know. I asked him if he loved her but he never answered me. I knew than he did not love her and I could not understand why he would marry someone he did not love.

After speaking with Edward, I put the energy that I used holding onto him into the relationship with Lloyd.

It is now November. Edward got married two months ago. Lloyd and I moved to St. Paul. This way at least I will not have to run into Edward with his new spouse. I don't think I could handle that yet.

Lloyd and my relationship over the pass few months got closer and closer. The feelings were changing daily. I found that I have fallen in love with Lloyd.

Things were great upon until March of 1990. Lloyd starts going out without me and sometimes would stay out until the next morning. One Friday I went to a Tenant Union meeting for our apartment complex. There I met a person by the name of Mary. Lloyd came to walk home together with me from the meeting. The next day I'm visiting Mary, she asked if Lloyd is my brother and I told her no that he is my significant other. She got a very strange look on her face and when I asked her why, she says: "Last weekend when I went out I met him. He approached me and asked if he could buy me a drink. We danced a few times and he asked for my phone number but I would not give it to him. He said he just moved here and did not have anyone." I did not get into it with her but left to confront him about and of course he lied. He denied that he approached her and him asking for her phone number. He said that she approached him. I did not take this conversation any further because he only denied doing it. He will eventually get caught, thinking to myself.

At the beginning of Spring Lloyd is ready to be free, saying: "I want to be free. I do not want to have to answer to anyone when I go out and stay to long." Lloyd and I broke up by the time May came around. I did not want to admit it but I'm miserable without him but refusing to let him know that he is able to put me in this state of mind. It is hard, but I never called or try to find out where he is living.

Two months passed and I have not seen or heard one word from Lloyd. I put my mind on my daughter and my job to keep from thinking about him. It got easier for me too not want to see Edward as months passed by. Until one night I ran across a box with photos of him and me when we were together. The photos remind me of the good times we had and now I want to know what Lloyd is doing. I called Lloyd's friend wife and she told me that Lloyd is living with a person on the south side of town. I sat down at the dining room table and poured a shot of cognac. The more I drank the madder I got. Finally I picked up the telephone to call the operator to see if Lloyd had a listed number. He did, so I called. Lloyd answered the telephone and I could tell he had been asleep. I said: "Hello, Lloyd." When he realized, it was I on the phone. He says: "Hi, How are you doing? And Why are you calling?" He is whispering and I knew someone had to be there with him, and now I have an attitude. I said: "You better get her out of the apartment because I'm on my way and if I have to I will kick the door in." I did not give him enough time to respond then hung up the telephone. I waited for fifteen minutes before calling him back. I dialed the number again and he answered again, saying: "Why are you tripping like this?" I interrupted him saying: "I'm on my way and she should not be there when I arrive." I hanging up the telephone again on Lloyd after I finished talking. I still did not allowing Lloyd to complete his sentence. I waited again for fifteen minutes and called him back again. This time she answered the phone and I asked to speak with Lloyd. She called for him but he did not answer. Then she said: "He must have stepped out." I told her: "You should have left with him because I'm on my way there and you better should not be there when I arrive." She hung up the telephone without saying anything. I called right back. The phone rang several times before Lloyd answered it and quickly said: 'She is packing her things to leave.' Why are you acting like this? 'If you had waited for another week, I would be coming home.' I replied: "Sure you were. Do you think I would really believe this lie?" Lloyd is crazy about money and she must be supplying him with plenty of it. I never intended to go to his apartment, I just wanted to see if I could yank his chain and now I know. I hanging up the telephone after I accomplished jerking Lloyd around. I vowed to never call Lloyd again. Lloyd letting the love for money dictates if our relationship is to continue then I need to move on with my life without him. Now satisfied and feeling no pain, I went upstairs to my bedroom and went to sleep. The cognac I drank made it easy to get a good night sleep, for a change.

Mom and I would walk to Mac Donald's every weekend in the morning for breakfast. We have become regulars there and acquainted with most of the employees. Especially, Stacey and she even called Mom, Mom. One morning she came over to the table. She is telling me of her boss' interests in me and wanted to get my telephone number. I did not think he is my type but from my other choice in men, I don't think I know what my type is. Stacey took it upon herself anyway to give him my telephone number after getting it from Mom.

On Sunday morning I received a call from Stacey's boss, Cliff. We talked for a half an hour before he asked if I would like to go out to dinner and a movie. I hesitated for a few seconds before I answered him. I accepted his offer. Cliff, picked me up about six thirty that evening. To my surprise, I had a great time with him. We had dinner at Red Lobster and to the movies afterwards. Cliff is polite, humorous, intelligent and fun. I found he quit interesting to be with. After a few more dates we begin seeing a lot of each others, every weekend at first and now every day almost. I needed him around as well as wanted him around. Cliff calls to see if he could cook dinner for me at his place. I had been there many times and he is always the gentleman, so I did not hesitate one second to take him up on his offer. It is just another date, so I thought. Cliff cooked while I'm watching television and sipping on a glass of wine. He came over to the couch to join me while dinner is simmering. We started out just playing around but it quickly turned into passionate kissing and holding. He is as gentle as if he is holding an expensive fragile porcelain vase and not wanting to drop it. We did not expect for this to happen but it did and it was great, like everything else he did. Cliff and I spent even more time together than before.

Only a month ago I had jerk Lloyd around and met Cliff, but it seems like six months.

Just when I thought, things with Cliff are getting heavy. I received a telephone call from Lloyd. He asked: 'How are you doing?' I knew by the sound of his voice something is wrong, so I asked: "Why are you calling me now?" He answered: 'I have been thinking about you and wanted to hear your voice.' I said: "Lloyd, be honest. What is wrong? You have not called in all this time, why now?" He explained: "The night you called and I told you I will be coming home. I was arrested because of some thing she was doing. I had been locked up for a couple of weeks and was too angry to let you know what had happened. While I was locked up all, I thought about was you and how I messed up what we had. It took this to happen for me to realize what I lost." I listened to him and all I could think about is the hurt he put me through. On the other hand I do still love him, but I love Cliff too. I asked: "What do you want from me now?" He answered: "Will you marry me?" I could not say a word because I'm in shock. He did not get an answer so he asked again: "Will you marry me?" I told him I had to think about it because he had treated me badly before and I'm not sure if I want to trust him now or ever. He is persistent and wanted an answer right than but I told him I could not give him an answer right now. He is angry and hung up the telephone. I dialed Cliff's number and when he answered I asked: "Is it possible we could have a future together?" He answered: "I hope to always have you in my life as a friend and I do love you but I'm not in love with you." I did not expect to hear Cliff say that and 'Boy'! Did it hurt? At least he is honest. After that statement, I told him I'm getting married, that an ex-boyfriend has asked but I have not given him an answer yet. He laughed it off as if I'm making a joke. We talked about it for a few minutes but he never took me seriously.

A week passed quickly, on January 4, 1992 Lloyd and I married. Cherry and her best friend Tonya were our witnesses and after the ceremony Lloyd went to move his things to my apartment. Lloyd is out picking up his things and now I can call Cliff to tell him that I just got married, saying: 'Congratulations are in order.' He asked: "What?" I answered: "I just got married today." He says: "You did not." I replied: "Yes, I did get married." Again, but now he realized I'm not kidding around. He says: "You did not do that to me. You did not." I replied: "To you, I did nothing to you. I'm still your fiend." I think this news is devastating to him. I asked him: 'Why did you not tell me the truth about how you really felt about me?' He answered: 'I had no ideal that you would really get married.' I could tell by his voice that he is really hurting. We talked for a few minutes more than I told him I will talk with him later. Now I'm angry at him because I realized than that I do indeed love him and would have loved to been his wife. It is too late now. I have married Lloyd.

Lloyd played the devoted husband for a few months and it was back to the real Lloyd. It is Friday night, Lloyd took a shower, dressed and headed for the door. He is showing all the signs of restlessness. He left about six thirty p.m. I have not heard from him since. It is now ten thirty p.m. I still have not heard for Lloyd. I took a bath and went to bed but could not go to sleep. Time is passing fast and the later it got, the more worried I had become. He still has not called home and it is now two o'clock A.M. I'm pacing the floor and now I well-passed worrying too mad. He could have at least called to let me know he is all right. It is seven A.M. My telephone rang. I answered it and Lloyd quickly says: 'Baby, I'm sorry, I'm stranded out in Minnetonka and have no way to get home until the buses' starts to run again.' Don't be mad. I will be home in an hour.' I quickly replied: "You don't have a home. Don't you dare come to this house?" He then says: "But Kay, it's not my fault. Where I am there are no phone and I had to walk a mile to get to this one." I just slammed the phone down. I'm really not in the mood to hear more of his lies. Later, I allowed him to come home. When he arrived, he went upstairs and packed his clothes, saying: "I did not want to get married in the first place." He said all kind of nasty thing to hurt my feeling and is doing a good job at it too. I began to cry and picked the luggage up and throw them out the front door as far as I could. When he went to retrieve them, I picked up one of my dining room chairs and throw it at him, hitting him in the back of his head.

Three weeks later, Lloyd called me back. I could not believe he had the nerve to ask me to let him come back home and most of all I could not believe that I let him come back. Our relationship ended and we are just going through the motions. We separated again and during this separation Cliff is back in my life. Cliff is a little apprehensive because he is not sure how Lloyd and I have left things. Cliff felt a little better about our relationship as time passed. I have fallen deeply in love with him. Lloyd would show his face every now and then just to see if he is still on my mind. Again I let him interfere with my relationship with Cliff. I refused to give up Cliff all at once, so we agreed to be friends. Cliff is angry that I let Lloyd back into my life but he did not hold it against me. Lloyd moved back in and after six months I became very ill. When I asked Lloyd to go with me to the hospital he replied: "You will be all right, you just need some fresh air and he got on his bike to his friend's house. He left me home sick. I called my Mom and asked her if she would come with me to the emergency room. She said yes and met me downstairs in a taxi. After we arrived at the hospital, the doctors saw me quickly because I'm not able to stand up without the help of someone and the color of my skin turned very pale. The doctors poked for hours on me. The doctor sent me to a different hospital to see a specialist so that he could find what they may have missed and could tell me more about what is happening with me.

The hospital is far from where I'm now and I needed to get their fast. Lloyd is no where to be found and I had no one else to call except Cliff. After I called and explained to Cliff what is going on and within ten minutes he arrived and drove me to the hospital. Cliff is concerned that he stayed until I saw the doctor. After a few minutes with the doctor, he sent me back to the hospital where I originally started from for emergency surgery. Cliff is so concerned that he stayed. drove me back and stayed. 'Cliffs' face is the last I saw before going into surgery.'

I opened my eyes after about six hours to Cliff standing next to me holding my hand. I'm glad he is still here. My Mom, Cherry and Barb were here with me too. I see no signs of Lloyd. I did not talk because I'm under the influence of the pain medication and fell into a deep sleep.

I woke with the sun shining in my face and to Lloyd's voice. Instead of him being concerned about my well being he is just starring at me with an angry look on his face. He did not say anything with the room filled with family and of course Cliff. I'm in and out of sleep but well aware of what is going on in the room. My Mom moved over to my bedside and kissed me on the forehead. She says: 'I am going homes now but will return early in the morning to stay with you.' Cliff leaned over and kissed me on the cheek and said: "I will be here later on to see you." Next Cherry appeared by my bedside, saying: "Mom, I love you and I will come back with Grandma tomorrow. You try to get some rest now." She hugged me and moved toward the door. Now there is only Lloyd here and when everyone is out of the room he moved close to me and says: "I don't want Cliff here at this hospital to see you again." I felt really weak but I sat up in the bed so that I could look Lloyd in the face. I said to him: 'If you had been home with me I would not have called Cliff but you had better things to do than coming with me to the hospital.' 'So don't you blame me.' 'Blame yourself for him being here.' With me saying this, he left and went home without saying another word.

The doctor released me seven days later to go home. I'm staying with my Mom because I need around the clock care and Lloyd has to work. Cliff came by and brought me some magazines, a card and some candy. He sat for a while until he had to return to work. Before he left, Lloyd showed up. He got upset again because Cliff is here. When Mom left the room Lloyd began fussing at me because Cliff was here and now he wants to take me home with him. He knows he cannot stay home but he insisted on taking me home so Cliff could not visit me. Lloyd packed all my things and took me home.

I have been home for two days and still not able to move about the house without assistance from him. I have to relay on him to run my baths, cook my meal and any other chores I'm not able to do myself. Then on Friday he says he wants to get out with his friends so he put everything close to me that I may need and left to get me something to eat. This is about six thirty in the evening when he left. I did not see Lloyd again until four o'clock a.m. the next morning and he crepes into the house, thinking I'm asleep and got into bed. I waited until he had gotten settled in bed and relaxed. I turned over enough to raise my arm high enough to get enough force and hit him right in the eye. He jumped up holding his face and did not ask why I hit because he knows why. He got a blanket and went to the living room to sleep on the sofa. He knew if he got back into bed I could reach him and I would hit him again. I pulled a stitch or two but it is well worth it. I took a pain pill and slowly dozed off to sleep.

It is morning and Lloyd is moving about the house getting ready to go to work. I decided that when he left I will call a taxi to take me back to my Mom's until I'm able to get around a little better. After two weeks at Mom's I'm feeling feeling strong enough to take care of business. I arrived home to pack my clothes and moved in with my daughter until I found my own apartment and that did not take very long. Again Cliff and I tried to get our relationship going but he is very cautious because I kept going back to Lloyd. Cliff did not want to get his heart broken again. Within a month's time I had gotten my apartment and back to work when Lloyd showed up at my door. Again begging me to take him back and again against my better judgment I let him in. Cliff became very disappointed and angry because I allowed Lloyd to mistreat me. Cliff, like myself having a hard time if he could not see me. We again agreed to be friends. It was only a short time after Lloyd had come back home that things were shaky once more. This time I did not put him out I dealt with him until I was sure it is over between us. What made it end for sure is when he had to go to court for traffic violations he receives while driving someone else's car. I went to court with him and found out who the car belonged to that he had been driving while separated from me. The car belonged to a female he met while separated from me. She appeared in the court room and giving me dirty looks as if I had done something bad to her. Finally she walks over to where Lloyd and I are sitting. I asked: "What is the problem?" She opened her coat to expose her stomach. She had to be at least five or six months' pregnant. She says: 'Yes, there is a problem.' 'I'm carrying his baby.' I replied back: "Then the problem is yours." She made a step toward me and I stood up quickly, saying: "If you have a problem with me we can take this outside." She stepped back and turned around returning to her sit. I looked over at Lloyd and shook my head. I finished up things here with Lloyd and walked out the door as fast as I could because if I had stayed close to him there is no telling what I would have done. I probably would have ended up in jail for knocking Lloyd in his head. Lloyd follows me but kept a little distance between us. He tried to talk to me but I'm in no mood to hear any of his lies.

When we arrived home, Lloyd and I both were silent for at least an hour. Then I had to ask the obvious question: "Is the baby yours?" He looked at me and said: "It is possible that the baby is mine but I cannot be sure." Then I asked: "Why didn't you tell me about this instead of letting me learn about this that way?" He answered: "I did not know if she was really pregnant until today. I thought she was just trying to break us up or trick me into coming back to her." I then asked: "What are you going to do? Are you going to be with her or with me?" He answered: "I want to be with you but I want to raise my child, if it is mine. I don't know for sure if it is my baby. I will have to see when the baby is born." I asked: "When is she due?" He said: "In October," Lloyd and I over the next three months did not talk about this situation much because there is always an argument. He knew as well as I did that this is the last straw. After the baby is born, our relationship got worst and I asked him to move out.

During the time that Lloyd and I were trying to work on our marriage, Cliff tried to move on with his life. Cliff got engage after a year passed to marry someone from his hometown. I had not talked with Cliff during the time Lloyd and I got back together because I wanted to give my marriage a chance to heal. I called Cliff shortly after I asked Lloyd to move out. The telephone rang for a few times before someone answered it and to my surprise it is a female answering the telephone. For a few seconds I became speechless, then I was able to ask: "May, I speak with Cliff?" She very politely says: "Cliff is not home, would you like to leave a message." I replied: "Would you tell him Kay called?" She then says in a different tone: "I will tell him you called." I hung up the telephone quickly. I don't know why it shocked me because Cliff is a good person and a great catch for any woman. I thought about calling him on his job but thought I needed to wait until he calls me, if he does. Within the hour my telephone rang and it is Cliff. After talking with him for about thirty, I realized that he is not happy with the relationship that he is in and has planned to end it as soon as possible. Cliff and my Mom are very close. He would take her to the casino, even when we were not talking. She considered him her son. Cliff and I even when he had broken off his engagement remained the best of friends. I cherish our friendship very much and would never do anything to ever jeopardize the relationship. Cliff has been there for me through my grand children's births, their birthdays and my countless hospital stays. He is there when no one else is and I love him for just being the person he is.

Edward was going through his divorce the last time I heard from him and he was seeing someone else. This was about four years ago. I will give him a call to see how the children are doing as well as he. Natalie answered the telephone. We talked and caught up with all that has happened in the pass few years. She told me that her father is overseas and been there for a year but she is expecting him home soon. I told her to tell him to call me when he gets home.

Once Lloyd found out about Cliff and things were not going the way he thought they should he would bring Cliff up in the argument. Lloyd is now using Edward. Lloyd would show up every blue moon just to see what I'm up to but when I told him that I have filed for a divorce the visit became less and less. He did not believe that I would divorce him until he showed up for one of his surprised visits and I gave him a copy of the divorce decree. He looked at and tore it in half. Lloyd asked before he leaves: 'Now, what is you going to do now, married Edward.' That is when I realized that Edward is the man that I want to spend the rest of my life with. It is just the matter of him wanting the same thing. I have loved Edward with all my heart and soul. I probably always will.

Chapter Five

Door number one, two, three and four are
made of wood and easily destroyed,
but door number five is made of steel and not
Too easy destroy and will last a lifetime.

I decided to give Edward a call and Natalie informed me that he is on his way back to Germany. So I will have to wait until he returns back to the United States to speak with him.

Cliff called me today to see if Mom and I want to ride with him to the casino. I told his yes. He will pick us up around eight p.m. I called Mom to let her know that Cliff wanted to take us to the casino and will pick us up at eight p.m. Mom is all for that. In the mean time I have chores around the house to do. Cliff called about seven forty five to let me know he will be here by eight fifteen. I have enough time to cook dinner for Mom and myself before he comes. Mom and I have just finished eating when the telephone rang. Cliff is down stairs. Mom and Cliff, teased me about grinning when in Cliff's present, the whole trip to the casino. This is what I had to dial with whenever the three of us are together. That OK because I know it is all for fun.

Mom knows that I care a lot for Cliff and she would tell him I grin so hard when he is around. Cliff is just as bad because when we are together we have so much fun and have a lot in common. This is very hard to find among friends or lovers. Cliff and I saw a lot of each others as friends even with him living with his fiancee. This went on for eight months or until Edward returned from Germany.

Edward returned home from Germany for a leave to go to Steven's graduation. He asked me to go with him, not knowing I'm part of Steven's graduation gift. I had not seen Steven in years. I'm also hoping this trip would be a romantic weekend for Edward and me. Well, romantic it wasn't but I enjoyed being with Edward anytime. I did get to see our granddaughter La Deja and spend time with Steven that was great.

Edward and I returned to Minneapolis on Monday morning that did not give us much time to spend with each other alone before he has to return to Germany. He did not seem concerned with spending any quality time with me. He will be leaving tomorrow night and will not be home again from Germany for at least five months.

After five months I called Natalie to ask when is she expecting her Father home, but to my surprise Edward answered the telephone. I heard Edward's voice and became excited and asked: "When did you get back?" He answered: "I was here for about nine days." I'm now angry because he has been home all this time and did not think enough about me to let me know that he is back in town. I said: "Welcome home, I will not keep you on the telephone but will talk with you later." Rushing to get off the phone with him because my attitude is change for the worst. I could not get it off my mind that he has been here all this time and did not call me.

I decided to call him back I needed to know if I'm again holding on to something that will never happen. Edward answered the phone. I asked: "Are you ready to be in a committed relationship?" Edward answered: "No, because I have lived with someone all of my adult life and I want to have sometime for myself." I understood. I did not like it but understood. I then said: "I understand but I'm not taking this on and off relationship into 1997. So, this is good bye and I would appreciate it if you would not call or come to see me ever again." I hung up the telephone not giving him any time to respond. It is December 29, 1996 at nine o'clock p.m. when my telephone rang. I looked on the ID caller to see who is calling and saw that it is Edward calling. I did not want to answer it because we have said all we needed to say to each other. My best friend, Charlene is here with me and she quickly picked up the telephone and answered it. I covered the receiver with her hand and trying to convincing me to take it. Finally I took the phone saying: "What is it you want?" He says: "I need to talk to you." I replied: "We do not have anything else to talk about." Edward insisted and I finally gave in. He arrived within fifteen minutes and as he entered the apartment Charlene left to give us some privacy. I asked: "What is it you want to talk with me about?" He asked: "Will you go to Florida with me?" I looked to see the expression on his face to see if he is serious and thinking: "Does he know what he is asking me?" I then asked him just that. He answered: "I know exactly what I'm asking you and before I move you to Florida, you will be my wife." You could have blown me away like a feather. I'm a little light headed and could not respond right away. I could not believe that the man who should have been my husband twenty years ago is now asking me to be his wife. He now wants to commit for life. I hid my feeling back because I did not want to get my hopes up to get them broken down again. Anything could happen before we actually get married. Edward could change his mind. Just to hear those words from him were like music in my ears. If it never happens at least, I heard him say the words.

Things were going so great, almost unbelievable great but also scary. Edward and I spent more and more time together planning our move to Florida and setting a date to be married. He will have to report to Jacksonville on the third of March that only gives us two weeks together before he leaves. Most of his friends congratulated us and most of them knew what was going to happen before I did.

It is March and Edward is in Florida but before he left, I move into his house with Natalie. Edward returned to Florida a month ago and I will leave to spend three weeks with him. I need to find a home for when I return in July. We made plans to get married in July. After I returned back to Minneapolis everything seems to start moving faster than before and Edward called to tell me he has made plans to come here on the twenty-third of April. He says: "We will get married on the twenty fifth." I'm finally beginning to believe it is really going to happen but still remain cautious. Edward told me to pick up the marriage license but I decided to wait until the day we are to get married to get them.

Edward arrived on the twenty third of April at eleven thirty p.m. and he arrived at the house by a taxi. I met him at the door with open arms. I kissed and hugged him. I'm glad he is home. We stayed up late talking and planning everything for Friday the twenty fifth. He has already informed the family members before he arrived here.

It is Friday, I went downtown to pick up the marriage license that took about two hours because the judge is still in court. I went to the courthouse to obtaining the marriage license from the judge and then I went home to prepare for the ceremony.

Edward and I got married finally and in the eyes of God, all of our family members that lived in Minneapolis and friends. Everyone is happy that Edward and I finally did it. Our children were the most thrilled. Everyone met over at Kelly's house for the reception. Nettie, made the first toast in our honor and then Walt, who is Edward's best friend.

Two days after the ceremony took place, we both heads to Jacksonville, Florida. We had the four children at home when we first met and now we are along together. We are very happy and enjoy our time together. Our children became independent adults with families of the own. David Joe lives in Fort Worth, Texas with his spouse and two children. Cherry lives in St. Paul with her spouse and three children. Natalie lives in Minneapolis with her spouse and two daughters. Steven lives in Iowa City, where he attends college.

Edward and I have been living in Florida now for four years. To this day, I'm still floating on cloud nine. My husband and I are best friends. I had to go through a lot to finally be able to be with the person that I have loved most of my life. It took me.

FIVE TIMES; THE BEST WAS LAST.

ABOUT THE AUTHOR

Kaysee Smalley,
Kaysee Smalley is presenting to us, her first work of nonfiction based on experiences of her life. The names, characters, places and incidents most were changed to protect the real-life counterparts. Other names, places and incidents are either the product of the author's imagination or used fictitiously and resemblance, if any, to the real-life counterparts.

www.ingramcontent.com/pod-product-compliance
Lightning Source LLC
Chambersburg PA
CBHW031239280526
45784CB00004B/1634